Praise for
CONGRATS! YOU'VE BEEN PROMOTED

"*Congrats! You've Been Promoted* is a crucial resource for today's emerging leaders, particularly in the wake of COVID-19, which left many young managers without traditional face-to-face mentoring. As experienced leaders retire and leadership gaps widen, this book steps in to provide essential guidance for those stepping into supervisory roles. It bridges the gap left by the lack of in-person training and mentorship, offering practical, real-world strategies to build confidence and effectiveness from day one. With actionable advice on communication, feedback, and conflict resolution, it's an indispensable tool for navigating modern leadership challenges and ensuring success in newly promoted roles."

—**Lucy Dunn**
CEO Emeritus,
Orange County Business Council

"A GUIDE for today's leaders . . . Noel has truly 'walked the walk.' In this book, he provides a clear and practical roadmap for becoming an effective leader in today's business world. Grounded in characteristics he cultivated, modeled and mastered over the arc of his impactful career, Noel's journey led him to become one of the nation's greatest business and civic leaders. Let this book put you on your path to exceptional leadership."

—**Matthew A. Toledo**
Publisher Emeritus
Los Angeles Business Journal
and CEO, ProVisors

"SOME LEADERS are full of theory and rhetoric. Noel Massie is not one of those leaders. In Noel's forty-plus years as a leader, mentor, and coach, servant leadership has been his mantra. Noel developed people by being intentional about how to lead and being granular in his approach. Noel's philosophy is that every interaction matters, and over time trust and respect is earned regardless of title. *Congrats! You've Been Promoted* dives deeply into the importance that in every connection all parties need to know exactly what is expected of each other and continuous feedback is the key. Terms and conditions can be the foundation to any organization's leadership culture."

—**Nicholas Kocheck**
President, Temco Logisitics

"Training people as they rise up the ranks and become managers can be challenging. This book provides very pragmatic lessons, examples, and activities people can use daily to manage better and to look at difficult situations in a new light. Noel has shared stories all of us can relate to; this book helps introduce management theory you learn in business school, but in a way that every person can grasp it and say, 'I can do that.' It's a great tool for leaders and those who want to move up in their corporations."

—**Renee Fraser**, PhD
CEO, Fraser Communications and
Radio Host of "Why Women," KABC-LA

"Noel Massie authoritatively, expertly, and engagingly outlines how to bring out the best in every employee and create effective, respectful, and resilient workplace teams."

—**Marc H. Morial**
President and CEO
National Urban League and
Former Mayor of New Orleans

"Every young aspiring leader benefits from having a mentor. There is no other mentoring book like *Congrats! You've Been Promoted*. Young leaders who read the book will benefit from practical guidance via examples from Noel Massie who discusses hands-on real-world experience in the book. This book will be particularly valuable to younger leaders new to a leadership position. Having been a college president, this book will truly benefit individuals who wish to work in academic administration including department chairs, deans, provosts, leaders of student affairs, and presidents."

—**Deborah Freund**
President Emerita
Claremont Graduate University

"NOEL SHARES even more wisdom and advice in this book, and I'm certain it will resonate with you, just as it has with me. It will empower you to lead with confidence, trust your instincts, and find the right words when it's time to speak up and lead."

—**Derrick Waters**
CEO, Coach U.S.A

CONGRATS! YOU'VE BEEN PROMOTED

An Essential Guide for Helping
New Leaders and Their Teams Succeed

CONGRATS! YOU'VE BEEN PROMOTED

NOEL MASSIE

former vice president of
operations for UPS

Foreword by Derrick Watters,
CEO of COACH U.S.A.

Congrats! You've Been Promoted: An Essential Guide for Helping New Leaders and Their Teams Succeed
Copyright © 2025 by Noel Massie

All rights reserved. No part of this publication may be reproduced, stored in a retrieval system, or transmitted in any form by any means, electronic, mechanical, photocopy, recording, or otherwise, without the prior permission of the publisher, except as provided by USA copyright law.

No patent liability is assumed with respect to the use of the information contained herein. Although every precaution has been taken in the preparation of this book, the publisher and author assume no responsibility for errors or omissions. Neither is any liability assumed for damages resulting from the use of the information contained herein.

Some names and identifying details have been changed to protect the privacy of individuals.

Published by Mission Driven Press, an imprint of Forefront Books, Nashville, Tennessee.

Distributed by Simon & Schuster.

Library of Congress Control Number: 2024926954

Print ISBN: 978-1-63763-399-1
E-book ISBN: 978-1-63763-400-4

Cover Design by Studio Gearbox
Interior Design by Mary Susan Oleson, Blu Design Concepts

Printed in the United States of America

To my mother, Ruth Alexander, thank you for giving your children a model of what hard work and persistence produces. To my wife, Amanda, and my sons, Pierce and Brayden, your support has meant more than I could ever state. To my ally Gary Medeiros, whom we lost too soon. He constantly pushed and challenged me to be the best person—let alone leader—I could be. To my many UPS partners and mentors, the lessons I learned from you are what inspired this book.

CONTENTS

FOREWORD 17
INTRODUCTION 21

PART ONE: *The Terms and Conditions of Values-Based Leadership* 37

CHAPTER ONE: Understanding Your Own and Your Team's Terms and Conditions 39
- When You Violate Another's Terms and Conditions 42
- In Every Aspect of Relationships, There Are Terms and Conditions 44
- There Are No Casual Moments 47
- You Never Get a Second Chance to Make a First Impression 49
- You Are Always Being Evaluated 51
- Meet the Influencers First 55
- One-on-One Meetings Establish Further Connection 59
- Four Steps to Establishing the Second Impression 65

CHAPTER TWO: A Fair Exchange 69
- What It Feels like to Be Treated Unfairly 74
- Exercises 90

CHAPTER THREE: Personal Ethics— Do the Right Thing 91
- Ethical Behavior: Are You Honorable? 92
- Just Because It's Legal Doesn't Make It Ethical 94
- Personal Ethics: The Buck Stops with *You* 102

- Exercises 109

CHAPTER FOUR: Listening—
A Skill or a Value? 111
- Why It Pays to Listen Empathetically 113
- Stop-Pause-Listen:
  Valuing Your Speaker 121
- Exercises 129

CHAPTER FIVE: Integrity—Your Crown Jewel. 131
- Integrity: A Core Value 134
- Day-to-Day Interactions
  Where Your Integrity Is at Risk 139
- Communicating Your Integrity Matters! 142

CHAPTER SIX: Trust 145
- Gaining the Trust of the Disgruntled, Bitter,
  or Anti-Establishment Employee 147
- Repairing Trust after
  You Have Broken It 152
- Exercises 155

CHAPTER SEVEN:
Providing Consistent Feedback 157
- Feedback Is More Than the Words
  You Speak 159
- Everyone Needs a Coach 165
- Exercises 169

CHAPTER EIGHT: Ownership
and Taking Responsibility 171
- Exercises 181

PART TWO: *The Fine Print: Putting Value-Based Leadership into Practice* .. 183

CHAPTER NINE: Building Employees' Skills and Keeping Your Team 185
- People Don't Quit Companies, They Quit People 190
- Training and Development 192
- Primacy: What You Learn First, You Remember the Best and Retain the Longest 195
- Know What You Don't Know, Then Get to Know It 198
- Exercises 202

CHAPTER TEN: Directional Communication 203
- Words Matter 203
- Comfort Matters 214
- Identify What's Holding You Back 215
- Practice, Practice, and Then Practice 216
- Exercises 218

CHAPTER ELEVEN: The B.E.S.T. Principle 219
- Exercises 226

CHAPTER TWELVE: The 4x5 Method 227
- Picking the Most Effective Point of View 229
- When to Use Various Viewpoints 230
- Levels of Intensity/Tone 232
- Definitions of Each Level 233

- Example of a Supervisor Using the 4x5 Method 235
- High-Gain or Open-Ended Questioning.....239
- Use Metaphors to Bridge the Gap 242
- Exercises...253

CHAPTER THIRTEEN: Daily Messaging with Your Team 255
- Daily Meeting Script Template..................... 263
- Step 1: The Attention-Getter 264
- Step 2: Tell Them What You're Going to Tell Them 264
- Step 3: Tell Them 265
- Step 4: Tell Them What You Told Them......266
- Step 5: Check for Understanding 267
- Exercises...269

CONCLUSION 271
ACKNOWLEDGMENTS................................... 279

FOREWORD

By Derrick Waters, CEO, Coach U.S.A.

My journey with Noel Massie began in 2005 when a mutual colleague introduced us. At the time, I wasn't working directly for him at UPS, but we got to know each other through a few casual meetings. It wasn't until 2010, when I started working under him, that I truly got to know him as a leader—and our beginning wasn't smooth. I thought Noel was tough. From the start, he made the ground rules clear. His words were direct, but looking back, they were exactly what I needed to hear.

Words matter.

Noel said this often. I had to learn it the hard way a time or two, but it stuck with me. Today, as a CEO myself, I recognize the importance of being intentional with my words and the power they hold. By the time you finish this book, I know you'll have your own favorite "Noel-isms"—those phrases he often repeated. One of mine is, "If it makes no sense, it's nonsense!" He's not wrong!

But it's not just the words themselves that matter. It is how we use them, when we use them, the tone we choose, and to whom we direct them. Noel made it clear that he was counting on me to deliver. Over time, I realized he wasn't just saying the words—he was willing to stand by them, and he stood by me. Within my first two weeks working with him, I could tell he was blunt and honest. He said what he meant, and that honestly helped me trust him. I knew I was working for the real deal.

You don't have to have work for Noel to gain all the wisdom, knowledge, and leadership skills he offers. In this book, he distills lessons from his decades as a leader at UPS into an accessible guide that you can easily apply to real-life settings.

As leaders, we need to do more than speak the words—we need to live them. Our ability to lead depends on it. If we want people to trust and follow us, they need to know that we stand behind our words. If Noel hadn't set the tone when I began to working for him, it wouldn't have been just bad for me and him—it would have been bad for UPS.

There was a lot at stake. I had just been given the opportunity to lead the largest engineering team at UPS as Director of Engineering. While I was already competent in my career, I had much to learn, as we all do when taking on new roles.

I quickly learned by example, especially from Noel. He took ownership of his actions—admitted when he was wrong and expected the same from his team. He also practiced what he preached. As a natural talker, I know it wasn't easy for him to become an active listener, but he did it through practice. This was something he and I worked on over the years—*Stop, Pause, and Listen.* Now, whenever someone comes to talk to me, I close my laptop and silence my phone. I want them to know they have my full attention, just as Noel did with me. I also give consistent positive feedback. Like Noel, I aim to find something positive to recognize in people daily. Even if you can't do this every day, simply practicing it will help you focus on the positive and help those you lead feel valued.

Today I lead 2,800 people. But when I started at UPS I was a C.O.D. Clerk (Collect on Delivery for all you younger folks!). From there, I worked my way up to Vice President of Operations for the Western US, overseeing everything from the Mississippi River to Alaska and Hawaii. And after serving as the COO of Coach U.S.A., I was promoted to CEO.

I have heard the words "congrats, you've been promoted" a few times in my career, and it always brings a mix of fear, trepidation, and excitement. *Can I do it? Will my words make a difference to those I lead?* The answer, as I've learned from Noel, is yes. One day, when I was feeling particularly discouraged, Noel looked at me with the direct honesty I'd come to trust and said, "Derrick, man, people want to hear what you have to say. You need to speak up." I did. And it made all the difference.

Noel shares even more wisdom and advice in this book, and I'm certain it will resonate with you, just as it has with me. It will empower you to lead with confidence, trust your instincts, and find the right words when it's time to speak up and lead.

INTRODUCTION

You've been promoted. Congratulations! The position you wanted is now yours. If you're like most people who choose this path, you probably have aspirations for a long career in leadership roles. This is just the beginning.

However, you'll soon find out that the euphoria of being promoted fades fast. Over time, people stop congratulating you as often and ultimately stop congratulating you at all. Why? As soon as you are given the job, things you never expected to have to manage, you now have to manage. You may have already found that there is no honeymoon period. Your boss and the people you are now leading expect you to know the job and to have their daily needs met—starting immediately.

There are constant demands and problems you will be required to lead a group of people through. There is no road map. You have to figure it out on your own. No one is waiting to show you how to lead a forty- or fifty-year-old, even when you are much younger than they are. You may also have to lead someone who comes from a culture you do not understand or know. This requires true leadership skill. How much skill you have in anything is directly connected to how much time you've spent developing that skill. And since you haven't been doing this leadership thing too long, you most likely haven't honed these skills. Yet you're still required to execute the tasks at hand.

So how do you acquire these skills? Who is going to teach you? I suggest that you find someone who has been exactly where you are and has current field experience—not just the theoretical kind that comes from books.

Now, I am not knocking books. They are tremendously helpful, and that's why I have written this one for leaders such as you. I have read lots of books about leadership—hundreds of leadership books, easily, during my four-decade career. A favorite passion of mine was searching for books on leadership and giving them to my direct reports. We'd read sections of them together and discuss a paragraph or

INTRODUCTION

two on a weekly basis.

The problem I have found with most books on leadership today is that they typically focus on developing high-level organizational dynamics for CEOs and presidents. These books are often written for those people looking to be the next Steve Jobs, Mark Zuckerberg, or Elon Musk, or for those who are looking for some secret method to becoming the next technology giant, entrepreneur, or guru of an industry. I rarely see books that focus on basic leadership principles for the leader who is newly promoted or who is often referred to as "middle management." There were even fewer of those books when I first got started.

If you are tasked with leading a group of people from whom you must get results while facilitating change, communicating directions, and promoting the company's core values and mission, then you are a leader. In the US alone, there are 21.4 million people in these types of leadership positions. Which means that while there are only five hundred Fortune 500 CEOs, there are over twenty-one million leaders working daily with little to no training in basic leadership skills. Think about that.

INTRODUCTION

I believe the first three to five years of a career in leadership are the toughest portion of the journey. It is the time when you know the least about what it takes to be a great leader, and yet you are tasked to lead anyway. It's sink or swim time.

WE NEED COMPETENT LEADERS NOW MORE THAN EVER

This book is intended for the individual who is new to a leadership position—any position that requires you to get results through others. When I was newly promoted to my first few positions in management, I went to the school of hard knocks to learn. There is some value to learning that way, no question about it. However, I never went to work so I could make mistakes and fail. The mere fact that I agreed and accepted a position to lead others means I was looking to be out front, setting the tone. I wanted that responsibility and accepted it, but I did not have a guide to leading at the entry level. Rarely did I see a book that focused on how to lead through the practical details of real-world situations that come up for supervisors.

INTRODUCTION

Today the daily grind of leading has become even more complicated for the supervisor than at any time in recent history. Changes in the world's political and economic climates challenge individuals, governments, and business leaders. One example is that during the pandemic, working from home became the norm, a practice that was not as relevant in the past. You now must have the skills to lead a team without constant contact. Today's social and political divisions rival that of the civil rights and Vietnam era of the sixties, which were some of the toughest times Americans have ever experienced. The emotions and opinions Americans have regarding the current conflicts across the globe come to work with them. Employees must work together while potentially having a distaste for each other. The leader must know how to keep them focused and working together.

WHY LISTEN TO ME?

In this book, you will learn how to lead a group of people to achieve the results that you ultimately are responsible for. I will use my personal journey through leadership to share with you the many lessons I have learned. Why am I the man for the job? Because I've been where you are. My first experience as a leader was at McDonald's when I was just sixteen years old. Shortly after being hired there in 1973, I was promoted to what was then called a crew chief. When I was eighteen years old, in 1975, I worked for IBM while I was a college student. I had the privilege of getting an internship with them during my freshman year, where I was assigned to a project group working on the development of the first laser printer. I was the lead lab technician overseeing a group of three interns.

In 1977, while I was still in college, I needed a job to pay for my education and went to work for UPS. Just three months after being hired, at only nineteen years old, I was promoted to a part-time supervisor position. I would be promoted within UPS seven more times. I completed my career at UPS in 2019 as the vice president of US delivery operations. I started my career leading a crew of four employees at McDonald's and ended up at UPS responsible for the output of over two hundred thousand people. I rose from an entry-level position as a worker while attending college to a president's position within a Fortune 500 company.

If you look at statistics on what good leaders look like and what criteria are used to judge their credentials early in their career, I fail on most, if not all, of the tests. Sixty-one percent of all senior leaders within Fortune 500 companies are white men; I am Black. The average height of males in leadership positions is five feet ten; in fact, most US presidents are almost six feet tall. I am five feet five. I grew up in East Oakland, California, in a working-class neighborhood. I don't have an Ivy League or other prestigious college education. My education was a patchwork—I went to two separate colleges to earn my bachelor of arts (BA) degree in business management.

There were many other barriers along the way. I could have allowed those to become impediments to my goals. I did not. I was fortunate and had mentors, male and female, of all races and backgrounds, who taught me how to stick to my goals and also how to lead effectively. I, however, had to be willing to learn and willing to listen to them and act on their guidance. And I did. My experience, drive, and openness served me well.

In addition to my career at UPS, I had the privilege of leading other groups in the community. I served as chairman of the board for the Los Angeles Urban League in 2011. In 2014, I was the chairman of the board for the Los Angeles Chamber of Commerce, the second largest Chamber in the nation. I was the first African American ever to serve as chairman of the board for that organization in their 125-year history.

I didn't get these assignments by accident. To this day, people call me to sit on boards and committees and ask me to lead teams for them. The reason is simple: They know I will get results. After a forty-plus-year career in leadership, I know how to get the job done. I know how to influence people.

The key point here to realize that in any leadership role the only thing you will be evaluated on by your team are your skills to lead. Your superiors will recognize that more than who you you are or where you came from. They want results from your team above all else. You get to control that by developing yourself.

INTRODUCTION

WHAT IS LEADERSHIP?

The more I grew as a leader, the more I began to see that leadership positions all had some things in common. An obvious similarity is that all of them require you to get results by motivating and inspiring people. **Leadership is the ability to influence others toward a common objective without coercion—no more, no less.** Good leaders influence positive outcomes; bad leaders spur negative impacts. As a leader, you decide the impact you want to have.

Leadership doesn't give a pass on the requirements to lead, regardless of the barriers. There are skills you must learn to be effective and to influence positive results.

Bottom line: When you were asked if you wanted the position, you said, "Pick me! Pick me!" Well, you were picked. This means the responsibility is on you to learn how to be an effective and influential leader.

Each time that I was promoted to a higher position, I had to learn the necessary skills and requirements to lead at that level. In essence, every time you are promoted, you are considered "new" and need to prove yourself. Why? No one leadership position comes with the same requirements or the same people as the previous position. The relationships I had with the groups I led drove my success—or lack of it. This was true 100 percent of the time.

THE IMPORTANCE OF GREAT MENTORS

The number one question I was asked after I achieved mid-manager status was, How have you been so successful? This came from people of different ethnic and cultural backgrounds, college students, and even professional colleagues. It wasn't lost on me that when people looked at me, they saw the obvious. Men who look like me are not typically people they were used to seeing holding my level of responsibility.

This was amplified when I became the vice president of US delivery operations. I flew often, usually three times a week. It was commonplace for the person in the seat next to me to strike up a conversation. They always asked me what I did for a living. When I shared my role with them, their surprised expression said it all. They didn't know me, so their reactions were based solely on appearance. My answer was consistent: "Luckily, I had good mentors, starting with my first-grade teacher when I was six years old, and throughout my career at UPS."

I did have exceptional mentors. They inspired me and pushed me to see beyond my own limitations. One especially significant and impactful person in my early years was my paternal grandfather.

My grandfather, who was born in 1900, taught me some key things about people. He was a barber and he also worked as a porter taking tickets on a passenger train. As a result, he was exposed to people from many cultures. When I was still a child, he'd say to me, "Your life will largely depend on your work ethic and the relationships you choose, so work hard and choose wisely." He would also say that people for the most part are the same. They want the same things. No matter what their skin color is or what country they are from, they want to be respected. They want to be able to make a living and to raise their family in safety. He saw a whole host of characters while he took tickets on the train or while cutting hair as a barber. Fortunately, he shared what he observed with me early in my life, and it has stuck with me to this day.

INTRODUCTION

EVERYONE HAS TERMS AND CONDITIONS

I found my grandfather's words to be true and relevant to all of the leadership positions I held. More importantly, I understood that even when I failed, all relationships have some set of standards or expectations inherent in them. From the day we are born, starting with our parents, relationships shape our futures. There are relationships we value and relationships we regret. There are unintentional relationships we find ourselves in that we want out of. There are intentional relationships we attempt to build, such as with our friends, our children, or our spouse or partner.

A fundamental truth is that all relationships have some form of terms and conditions attached to them. Most leaders, however, generally disregard the personal aspect of this when interacting with their people. They believe the employee has a relationship with the company or that they are being paid to do a job. Phrases such as "Keep it to business as this is not personal" or "Leave your problems at the door" permeate company cultures. The problems I found with these statements were twofold. Number one, an employee's job is generally, after their family, the most personal thing in their life. Secondly, the company may employ them, but *you* lead your team. To the employee, you *are* the company. Everything they believe the company is doing to them, good or bad, they will ascribe to you, their immediate supervisor. Employees have expectations, and these are their terms and conditions of employment. If you fail to meet them, they will fail to do good work. If they fail, then you fail. It's not complicated.

This book will teach you how to understand that terms and conditions do exist for all individuals and within their workgroups. You will see how you can lead in a way that acknowledges the basic nature of an individual's psychological yet unspoken requirements. You will recognize how to identify your team members' personal terms and conditions, all for the purpose of getting the very best from them.

The terms and conditions of values-based leadership I will talk about in this book are:

- Treating people fairly
- Engaging in ethical behavior
- Listening well
- Maintaining integrity

- Earning trust
- Communicating and giving effective feedback
- Taking ownership and personal responsibility
- Building your team and retaining employees

To effectively lead, you also have to navigate real-world and real-life demands—which I call "the fine print"—such as:

- Building employees' skills
- Training and developing your team
- Offering directional communication
- Motivating your team

Finally, understanding cultural, ethnic, political, gender, and generational differences are critical in navigating today's climate. Men don't lead only all men, women all women, Black people all Black people, white people all white people. The skills you must possess early in your career impact all groups and people equally—they are valued by all. I've led multicultural groups over the course of my entire career.

In this book, I will use personal examples I've witnessed, experienced, and navigated over six decades of life. I will also provide some exercises to complete that will help you successfully build your skills. If you are in a leadership position, you have probably already discovered that your success is directly related to the attitude and skill of your team. The ways in which you daily coach, understand, and treat your team impacts their willingness to support you and your organization's goals.

Let's get started.

PART ONE

THE TERMS AND CONDITIONS OF VALUES-BASED LEADERSHIP

CHAPTER ONE

UNDERSTANDING YOUR OWN AND YOUR TEAM'S TERMS AND CONDITIONS

My 2011 BMW has 139,000 miles on it. The warranty expired after 50,000 miles and, as a precaution, I purchased extended protection. I'd owned four BMWs prior to this one, so I knew that any future repairs could be very expensive. It seemed like a sound decision to buy the policy. As it turns out, the car needed three separate significant repairs that ran thousands of dollars. Each time the service adviser contacted the company that sold me the warranty, and each time they denied covering the repair. I followed up on each occasion with the warranty holder, and each time they let me know that under the agreement the repair was not a covered item.

After the third time, I became extremely agitated and canceled the policy. Shortly after that, I received a call from a salesperson asking me why I had canceled. I shared the stories with them about none of my repairs being covered, and the salesperson asked me, "Well, did you read the fine print within the terms and conditions completely upon purchase?" With that question, I politely ended the call and asked them not to call again.

The fact is, I had *not* read the terms and conditions completely, and I certainly didn't read the fine print. I had skimmed through them as I always do with everything I purchase. I mean, who *actually* reads the complete list of items in the terms and conditions of the stuff they buy? After I read the policy, I saw that, of course, they were correct. The policy stated what would be covered and what would not be covered. The company wanted to ensure that you knew they would only cover faulty parts, not normal failure associated with wear and tear. They also wouldn't cover anything associated with improper use. That made sense. For example, were I to drive the car through a river, which that car is not meant to do, why should they repair it?

UNDERSTANDING YOUR OWN AND YOUR TEAM'S TERMS AND CONDITIONS

From that day forward I began paying attention to the phrase "Terms and Conditions" relating to any item I purchased. I began to read them in their entirety—even if it took an hour! Everything I bought had terms and conditions, whether it was a purchase from an app store or a new appliance for my home.

The primary focus of all terms and conditions is this: If you use an item for something other than what it was made to do, you shouldn't expect it to work as intended and it might stop working altogether. I later began translating that toward leading people.

In the introduction, I listed the values that form many of the expectations employees have of their leader. These are the values-based areas that form most of the terms and conditions we have as individuals. In every activity you have been engaged in during your life that involved another person, there were terms and conditions within the relationship. You most likely didn't treat them as if they existed in such a conscious way, but they were there, implied.

When someone's terms and conditions have been violated, you can expect them to react unfavorably. When you hire an employee, you are buying their time and energy. In other words, you made a purchase, and with that came their terms and conditions. If you abuse or misuse them, as with anything else you purchase, they will not behave or perform in a way that you anticipated.

WHEN YOU VIOLATE ANOTHER'S TERMS AND CONDITIONS

My family and I were taking a vacation in 2004. Our flight was booked from Norfolk, Virginia, to Lake Tahoe, California. We lived outside of Richmond, and the airport in Norfolk was about a two-hour drive from our home. It just so happened that our flight was leaving on the day when the clocks were moved ahead by one hour.

When we realized we had not factored in the time change, my wife and I knew we were likely to miss our flight. Our sons were looking forward to the trip and had been discussing it all week. In a last-ditch attempt to make the flight, I hurriedly packed the car, and my family and I drove for two hours to Norfolk. We arrived at the airport with minutes to spare. The ticket counter agent called the departure gate to inform them we were coming.

A disaster had been averted! However, when we arrived at the gate, the agent informed us that they had given two of our four seats away. I was incredulous with the agent, raising my voice and exclaiming, "How could you do that?" The agent attempted to calm me down, but I went on and on. Then, without so much as a word, she turned and walked away.

My wife calmly intervened and handled the situation by rebooking us for another flight the following day. It was so clear I had violated that employee's terms and conditions. As a result, she ceased helping me. I had purchased four plane tickets as well as her time to provide assistance. That is all true. However, she did not sell me her dignity. By amplifying my voice and raising the intensity of the moment, I was improperly using her services. So she simply left the situation and quit on me. If I had been her, I would have left me there too!

When employees are hired, they expect to be given a fair opportunity. This starts with fair treatment. They expect to be spoken to with consideration and dignity. If treated unfairly, they will respond by providing poor work, and just like the ticket agent did, they will check out emotionally as a means of self-preservation. When this happens, they are not checking out on the company, they are checking out on you! This happens when their terms and conditions have been violated. It's easy to do and difficult to correct. The prudent leader will understand that building positive relationships is necessary to produce positive outcomes.

IN EVERY ASPECT OF RELATIONSHIPS, THERE ARE TERMS AND CONDITIONS

Your spouse or partner, your family, and your friends all have terms and conditions. And if you're a leader, your employees have them. They are generally unspoken; nevertheless, it is your job to figure them out and to adhere to them. All individuals have feelings that connect them to any relationship they have.

When someone is treated in a way that they find unacceptable, their behavior reflects this treatment. They will not perform according to your expectations if they are not spoken to with

dignity. This respect was implicitly agreed on when they were hired.

The chapters ahead are designed to help you understand the basic terms and conditions that exist for all individuals within workgroups. They will demonstrate how you can lead in a way that acknowledges them. The following chapters will also help you identify your team's terms and conditions as well as each individual team member's terms and conditions. If you want to get the best out of your employees, the place to start is by understanding their terms and conditions.

The values we discussed in the introduction, which we will be breaking down in the following chapters, aren't complex. We all deserve fairness. Who wants unfair treatment? Who wants to be disrespected? Who wants to be blown off when they are speaking?

If it's so easy, you may wonder, why do so many leaders and teams have so many issues? I believe there are two reasons: a lack of understanding of the terms and conditions, and a leader's unwillingness to learn them.

I have a plaque in my office that reads, "Leaders act in ways consistent with their beliefs." A great leader I worked with over twenty years ago gave that plaque to me and several of the managers in our group. In other words, leaders can't say they care about being ethical and then behave unethically. They have to be willing to walk the walk. To achieve consistent behaviors, a leader must be intentional in commitment to them. In the pages ahead, we'll take a deep dive into those values and behaviors.

And it starts on day one of being a leader.

Consider the following and write down the terms and conditions that were violated in each instance:

- Think of a time when you experienced a situation with a boss that left you the most deflated emotionally.

- Recall a personal situation where a simple misunderstanding dramatically impacted a relationship.

- Reflect on a situation where you were doing business with someone and they failed to live up to your or your company's expectations.

THERE ARE NO CASUAL MOMENTS

When I was first promoted at UPS, I was assigned to lead nine employees. I interviewed for a position in leadership on a Friday. When I reported to work the following Monday, I was informed that I had been promoted! My supervisor congratulated me and let me know that I was starting immediately. I was expecting something more formal. The promotions I had witnessed appeared to be followed by various meetings and trainings and seemed as if they took weeks to complete. I certainly wasn't expecting a battlefield promotion.

I reported to the area I would be leading. A few employees were in the area, and they acknowledged my arrival with nods of hello. There were no words exchanged among us. I waited patiently for my supervisor to introduce me to them officially. While we were all waiting, they were wondering who their new supervisor would be. Some were stressing over the mystery of what that person would be like. The supervisor I was replacing had developed a very strong relationship with them. I stood there dressed exactly as they were. (Remember, I hadn't known I was being promoted.) I simply stood there and listened to them. They assumed I was there to cover an absent employee for the night. They believed they were speaking out of the listening range of management.

My supervisor arrived and asked the group to assemble and introduced me as their new supervisor. The employees looked at me with surprised expressions on their faces. I had stood there for at least five minutes and had not introduced myself. It was even more damaging that I had listened to them discuss their concerns about their future supervisor. One of the employees made this comment to me before going to his work assignment: "Oh, so you like being sneaky." Forty-two years later I can still picture that moment clearly. I had been their supervisor for five minutes, and in that span, I had created—at least in some of their minds—doubt about whether I was trustworthy. This would haunt me for months with this group, and building relationships with them would prove difficult.

Whether you are a new supervisor, manager, or CEO, you are "new" each time you get promoted. I always hated being new. The word itself suggests to those around you that you are inexperienced and don't know what you're doing. This is true—you *are* inexperienced in the new role. So the people under you will be evaluating everything you say and, more importantly, every action you take. This never changes. However, in the beginning of your new assignment the scrutiny is amplified. The challenge leaders face, especially early in their careers, is that this investigation is not obvious or a priority. New leaders instead tend to believe "I must be good. I must be smart. After all, I was promoted." They ignore the first step one must take when promoted to lead a team: the introduction.

This is where you get to give your team some knowledge of who you are. It is arrogant to believe your team doesn't need to know you or your values in order to follow you. They will immediately start sizing you up. There are no casual moments.

YOU NEVER GET A SECOND CHANCE TO MAKE A FIRST IMPRESSION

First impressions are lasting. They stick. Good first impressions can open the door for relationships. Bad first impressions, while not a death blow, make building relationships far more difficult.

As a new supervisor, you need to plan how you intend to introduce yourself to your team and each member of it.

In the beginning of any relationship—a first date or meeting the parents of your partner for the first time, a job interview, applying for credit—you go to great lengths to make a great impression. Being promoted to lead a group of people who do not know you is *exactly* the same scenario. You should be putting your best foot forward. The employees want to get to know you just as much as you want to get to know them.

Repeatedly I had to remind newly promoted individuals not just to dive into the reports and results of their new team. I urged them to focus on the people in that team first, to get to know the individuals. They wanted to hit the ground running, which is a good thing. However, results don't come from reports; they come from the people being motivated to support the leader. An appropriate introduction requires preparing a narrative regarding who you are and expressing your commitment to your team. The beginning of a relationship is your greatest opportunity to establish the terms and conditions that will manifest between you and the team.

YOU ARE ALWAYS BEING EVALUATED

My first manager, Glenn Libbrecht, was an excellent coach and leader—the true definition of one. He constantly reminded me and all of the supervisors under him, "You are always being evaluated." You never get to have a neutral moment with people, at work or otherwise. Leaders are not free from being evaluated.

In Malcolm Gladwell's bestselling book *Blink*, he discusses how our subconscious mind works when making assessments of all things. He calls it "thin-slicing." For example, when you see an approaching dog and it is snarling at you, you recognize the danger in an instant and react, no deep thinking required. An impression was made, and it sticks every time you see that dog or a similar dog. When someone you don't know approaches you with a big smile on their face, you recognize friendliness and react accordingly. Thin-slicing is when you make assessments quickly and subconsciously—in the blink of an eye. These assessments aren't within a person's control. When they are having a "blink moment" they make a hasty judgment. If you give your people an initial negative blink moment, they will remember it and will use it to judge you. The same holds true for a positive blink moment.

In the story I provided earlier, when I didn't introduce myself for five minutes, my new team had evaluated me and had their blink moment. They formed opinions about me, including that I could not be trusted, because of that experience.

There will be nothing you say or do as a leader that doesn't have a consequence. If you say selfish things, your team will react accordingly. If you say positive and inclusive things, they will react accordingly. You have the power to create positive blink moments, or negative ones, but it is your choice.

There is one thing everyone gets to control each day: their own behavior. This is an inarguable statement. Everyone has the discretion to decide what they do and how they do it.

In 1987, I was a manager assigned to lead a group of fifty-three delivery drivers in California. After being assigned, I had an introductory meeting with my new manager. In that meeting, he began to review with me the metrics, or key performance indicators (KPIs), of the operation. What stood

UNDERSTANDING YOUR OWN AND YOUR TEAM'S TERMS AND CONDITIONS

out the most were excessive daily complaints from customers. This group was generating nearly twice as many customer complaints as the average unit. He wanted me to correct that quickly. I had yet to meet the employees, and he was reviewing with me all of the unacceptable metrics within the unit. Not once did we discuss any employees. This was a routine approach then and still is today.

Results come from individuals, not from looking at reports. The first meeting with my new manager would have been more effective if we'd focused on the people. For instance, who was excellent, who needed additional training, what members of the team were participating in any of the many local committees? We had safety, service, and employee recognition committees in all units. This is pertinent information I would have benefited from knowing prior to meeting my new team.

After the meeting, I made a plan where I would spend at least thirty minutes a day speaking with just one employee. In these meetings, the employees and I would talk, engaging in a two-way conservation. The tone of the conversation would be to allow them to talk more than me, which is difficult for me to do! The intention I'd set for the conversation was to allow me to learn how they felt about their jobs, what issues they were having, and how I could help with those issues. In addition, I wanted their opinion on the customer complaint issue and how they believed we could correct it.

I understood the principle a previous mentor had taught me, to *know what you don't know*. He explained that knowing applied to people, not just problems. By meeting the employees in this intimate way, I would get to know something about them. Employees are as capable of analyzing and solving problems as anyone in management—they do the actual work! They always know what the problems are and, more importantly, what they would do to fix them. Ignoring these capabilities can have negative consequences. "Don't ask, don't tell" doesn't work in a leadership position; you want to ask and you want them to tell.

You must keep in mind that your employees, when they are not at work, might be leaders themselves. They may be coaches for Little League, run groups at their church, be members of city councils. Many are parents, one of the toughest leadership positions there is!

Additionally, some employees may want lots of overtime, but other employees won't want any overtime as they value being home more than being at work. Some could have an elderly parent they care for, or perhaps a parent with Alzheimer's or dementia. They may be taking classes in the evenings. To lead a team effectively, you must allow yourself to get to know them.

When asked, most employees will share what they want you to know. You won't have to probe for much of this information. My experience in this regard has been consistent. Leaders who believe they are more intelligent than their people are both ignorant and arrogant.

MEET THE INFLUENCERS FIRST

The term *influencer* is very popular today. There are individuals with a social media presence so powerful they have companies advertising on their sites. But long before the modern social media boom, the term *influencer* was used in leadership circles.

Employees are influencers as well. I was taught

early in my career about the importance of identifying workgroup influencers. The reason is similar to that of social media: They help spread messages. The first meeting I held with the delivery driver group was with the union steward, a key influencer. He and I spent the entire day together while he delivered his route. He was the person employees went to when they needed to voice complaints and concerns. He had a keen sense of the group's overall tone and sentiments.

I made him aware I'd be spending the day with him prior to doing so. Why was this important? If I had shown up and surprised him with no notice, he might have found me intimidating and untrustworthy.

By letting the employee know ahead of time that you'll be with them, you are able to express your intentions. You are also giving the employee an opportunity to think about what they would like to discuss. As an influencer, they will most likely broadcast to the group the news that you will be with them. This allows you to begin establishing trust and to make future discussions with others feel more natural.

When spending time with your employees, you want to set the tone. Opening with small talk puts the employee at ease. Simple, nonconfrontational questions are the best lead-in. There are, however, dos and don'ts when you are in these introductory meetings.

DOS

Begin the session by creating small talk to set a positive tone. Use open-ended questions that require more than a yes or no answer. For example, What are your hobbies? Discussing sports and community volunteerism are generally safe topics to open with.

Share information with the employee that they may not be aware of, such as up-and-coming innovations that your company is pursuing. I often sought out information before the meeting so that I could share what I knew about the company's plans. Doing so helps employees recognize the role they play in the organization and how their work impacts the company as a whole. It also helps remind them why you are all there in the first place—not just to make a living. It creates a sense that each employee matters to the big picture and their roles have a real purpose and impact. You can also share company wins, such as when customers are satisfied and appreciative. Let employees see that you appreciate their work and contribution. And request the ways you can better support them.

DON'TS

Avoid getting too personal. Don't delve into areas that you yourself would not want to discuss. Marital status and child issues are taboo. If these topics come up, don't engage. Gently change the subject. You are the employee's supervisor. You are not a social worker and should never give personal advice.

Don't get baited into agreements or make any major changes the employee is asking for. Do your research first and always follow up on the issue. When you are new you will hear all types of gripes, grievances, and requests for changes. It's normal. Don't get into debates about controversial company issues. Just tell the employee you'll take note of their feelings and share it with your superiors. This session is meant to be geared toward meeting the employee—keep it on track. You don't want to compromise your credibility.

DEFINITELY DON'T

The worst thing you can do is show up with an approach that insinuates messages such as:

"I am the boss, and you'll do as I say!"

"You're here to serve my needs."

"Your opinions aren't important."

DEFINITELY DO

Remember, your goal is to establish the terms and conditions between you and your team. Follow-up is critical. You have spent the time with them, and your follow-up begins establishing trust.

Listen to their concerns.

Write down the feedback you receive from each employee.

Review with your immediate manager areas where you feel their advice is needed.

ONE-ON-ONE MEETINGS ESTABLISH FURTHER CONNECTION

I currently mentor six individuals ranging in ages from twenty to mid-thirties. Recently, one of my mentees, Jenny, was reviewing some issues she was having in her group of twenty-seven employees. At the time, she had been their leader for a little over two months. A few of her employees were taking up the majority of her time, intentionally and daily. They would complain about any decision that was made, whether by her, her boss, or the company. These included routine assignments, goals—you name it. If she gave any instructions directionally or shared a policy update, this small group would complain. She always committed to following up and trying to keep the peace with them. A pattern developed. Every day she spent a significant amount of her time seeking answers to their questions. This had become an issue for her.

I shared a few examples with Jenny of employees who had done exactly the same thing to me early in my career.

"What are your priorities daily?" I asked.

She spouted off a number of things. None involved spending one-on-one time with any member of her team.

"Jenny, results come from individuals, not reports," I said.

I then asked her to tell me something personal

about her employees. She had very little information.

"You have not met your people on their terms as individuals," I said.

She agreed; she had not.

She then gave me a number of barriers she faced daily for not meeting with her people: for instance, not enough time, scheduling was challenging, and company meetings were often spontaneous, making planning difficult. So I said, "Leaders do what is important for them to do. *Your people see you loud and clear.* They see that they aren't very important to you. As a result, they are setting their terms and conditions. If you make no investment in knowing your people, don't expect them to make one toward understanding your true responsibilities."

I further explained that she couldn't expect to be supported by her employees if she didn't support them. Employees who need daily attention are going to be certain they get it.

"Either you're going to spend a lot of time managing small conflicts or you can spend the time getting to know them individually. Choose which one of those you want. The barriers you mentioned are not going away. Every individual has different buttons to push to achieve work satisfaction," I said.

As their leader, Jenny needed to be aware of her people's buttons. You can only know that by talking to someone personally. After our discussion, she developed a plan to identify the influencers first and begin meeting with her team members one-on-one.

We covered the dos and don'ts that Jenny would adhere to in her meetings. I encouraged her to make a list, something she could hand to the employee as a guidepost for the discussion. Since that was the first time she'd be engaging in this process, I let her know that this method would help to keep the conversation on task. She wanted to avoid allowing a gripe session to occur.

When questions are prepared prior to the meeting and written down, the employee is more likely to stay within those parameters.

Jenny would be setting the terms and conditions for the meeting. Additionally, I suggested that she practice or role-play a meeting with a friend or colleague. Rehearsing prior to a meeting leads to comfort during the meeting.

A couple of weeks later we met again. Jenny reviewed the meetings she had held with her team.

UNDERSTANDING YOUR OWN AND YOUR TEAM'S TERMS AND CONDITIONS

In those meetings, she followed the dos and don'ts we'd discussed as well as the terms and conditions she wanted them to know about her as their leader.

Jenny spent the most time engaging with her staff about the topics of respect, fairness, honesty, and integrity. She did this in order to solidify the expectation of professionalism from each member of the team. During the conversations, she also mentioned that she wanted them to speak first and the most. She only asked questions for clarity and follow-up purposes.

We also discussed the importance of making an employee feel and understand that this was *their* meeting. The meeting was the time and place for them to let her know everything they wanted her to know. Jenny was excited and enthusiastic about what had been accomplished in those sessions. The tone of her day and the tone with her group had changed dramatically.

When we wrapped up, I asked her to tell me one profound lesson she had learned.

"I learned that knowing my people personally helps me lead them better and it helps me professionally, and that it matters, and it matters a lot," she said.

Whether you've recently been promoted or not has little bearing on the need to reflect on key points I have discussed in this chapter.

You will have two opportunities to make a first impression: once with the group and once individually.

First you will meet the group as a whole and make a first impression.

In individual meetings, you will have an opportunity to build on that first impression with each employee.

Second impressions happen one-on-one with individuals and can have a massive impact. How often have you heard someone say, "You know, I spent some time with Susan, and she's a lot different than I thought she was!"

A relationship between two individuals cannot be accomplished in a group. Think about the first time you attended a family gathering with your partner. Your partner introduced you and said, "Hi everyone, I'd like you to meet John." If they are anything like my family, whispers began with questions such as, What does he do? How did they meet? What do his parents do? On and on. This reaction is normal; your team will do the same thing. As such, if you don't take the initiative to create the second impression, it will create itself—you get to control that.

FOUR STEPS TO ESTABLISHING THE SECOND IMPRESSION

Develop a plan to get to know each member of your team. As the saying goes, "A failure to plan is a plan to fail." If your first interaction has come and gone, there are four steps to establishing your second impression.

1. **Plan the introductions you will give to each team member prior to meeting with them.** Prepare a message where you will communicate the principles and ground rules that you'll abide by as their leader. Develop and write the meeting guidelines you will hand to them before or during the session so they will know what to expect. During the first few weeks build a daily communication framework that reinforces these messages. This holds you accountable to them, and them accountable to you.

2. **Meet with each team member individually.** This is your chance to establish the terms and conditions you want within the group. Discussing values such as respect, professionalism, and integrity helps you to set a professional tone. How long it takes for you to complete this cycle is less important than your team's knowledge that you will be taking the time to meet them as individuals.

3. **Write down all feedback.** Review how each person thinks and feels. This will open the door for you to begin moving in a direction where the concepts of terms and conditions can be utilized.

4. **Follow up.** The most critical step is the follow-up. The follow-up discussion should be five to ten minutes within a week of the session. This further signals to your team that the values you discussed in the session matter. It also communicates that their thoughts and input are important.

You can and most likely will shape and shift your leadership style with experience. While getting to know the individuals, listen to their feedback closely. They will communicate to you consciously and subconsciously what their terms and conditions are. Your role is to listen and observe closely while they speak. Success won't come if you fail to acknowledge the core expectations of individuals. They expect respect, fairness, honesty, and integrity from their leader.

CHAPTER TWO

A FAIR EXCHANGE

When I started my career, I didn't know all that I do now about what it means to be a leader, but I did know that I wanted to be a fair leader. I often recall what the founder of UPS, Jim Casey, said about fairness: *To give or get what is required in accordance with equal exchange doesn't call for tricky schemes or methods. Quite the contrary, if we resort to any such schemes our people will see it. As a result, they will give us a really hard time.*

However, I soon learned that what is fair to an individual or group is all about perspective. There are many components to fairness, and as a leader, you must have a firm grasp of that. A perfect example of this is the various opinions on safety people had during the 2020 pandemic. Some thought being required to wear a mask was fair. Others saw it as patently unfair. The same was true for being vaccinated. Many felt that being told what to inject into their bodies was unfair.

The pandemic was a somewhat extreme situation because it was unprecedented. Nobody's opinions were necessarily right or wrong. It was up to world leaders to understand and try to respond to different perspectives on fairness. Leaders in companies must do the same for their employees.

As a leader, I believe fairness is one of the most important traits your team will use to evaluate you. Understanding fairness, as a concept, will help you be fair in your dealings with others.

What is fair is routinely questioned by employees, whether it is a company policy change or your treatment of individuals. We all have a natural inclination to show favoritism. When employees excel and do good work, they become a leader's favorites. Excellent employees require the least amount of guidance, and they tend to be the ones a leader gravitates toward. They are typically agreeable and easy to lead.

Conversely, those employees who require more effort become "disfavored," and a leader strays away from them.

Your challenge as a leader will be to make sure all your employees consider you to be fair and unbiased. They all expect to be respected, listened to, and treated fairly. How you live the values of the terms and conditions of leadership must be equal to all.

Favoritism has been defined as "the practice of giving unfair preferential treatment to one person or a group at the expense of another." Statements such as "Life is not fair," "To be fair," "That's not fair!" and "Fair play!" are phrases that get to the emotional root of how important fairness is to people. It is highly valued. The view of what is seen as fair starts for most people during childhood.

I have two sons, Pierce, who is twenty-nine, and Brayden, who is twenty-seven. Growing up, they both always compared gifts that my wife and I gave them. This is natural for children. My older brother, Tony, and I also compared gifts. Anyone with siblings experiences this. As parents, my wife and I had to diligently keep track of all gifts so as not to create a perception of favoritism. We still engage in this practice today. If we give one of our sons less than the other, they create a mental IOU for us. Children have a fairness radar. It's not just with tangible gifts but with behaviors such as attention, love, and devotion.

Fairness also includes the interpretation of rules. My older son, Pierce, played Little League baseball when he was twelve. He never missed a practice. He felt that was important. Yet he played sparingly in games. Other players would miss practice and get to play the entire game. Yes, they were better athletes. The coach, however, had a bias. Coming to practice did not matter to him. His players saw that and acted accordingly. Those who didn't have to practice didn't, and there were no consequences. Those who had to practice did so, but there was no reward for all their efforts. After a while, it's easy to say, Why bother?

Today Pierce is a doctor. I am sure he has seen a lot of unfair acts in his day, but if you ask him when he was treated the *most unfairly*, he still points to that Little League experience. People do not forget when they experience what they believe to be unfair treatment. Most of us can relate and have a primary experience of being treated unfairly that still triggers us.

Make no mistake: Employees remember when they were treated unfairly and keep score. And they will measure you as the leader by their perception of fairness. Your employees will watch how you react to others and what you do for each person within the group. Which employees do you talk with the most? Who do you laugh with? Who do you spend time with off the job? When they see you go the extra mile for one employee on an issue versus others, they will see it as favoritism. When the leader shows favoritism to anyone, the group sees it clearly, even more so than the leader does. Remember, you're always being evaluated.

When being assigned to lead a workgroup, you most likely will find that there are customs and agreements in place—namely, the agreements the prior leader had developed with some or perhaps all of the employees. They won't be official policies or written rules. Rather they will be customs outside of official policies and written rules. However, these "unwritten rules" will mean as much to the employees as official ones. In some cases, these can compromise the organization.

These unofficial customs are often exposed when a change occurs: a new supervisor is installed, or an employee is transferred into a group.

A phrase I coined and used often when mentoring leaders was "Keep the lines straight," meaning don't make your own rules, and follow the guidelines we have. If you want to change a procedure or policy to make it better, there is a proper way to make recommendations to those who hold higher positions than you in companies. Don't make those changes yourself without following the guidelines. Going outside of the lines can have unintended consequences.

Fairness requires keeping everyone on an even playing field.

WHAT IT FEELS LIKE TO BE TREATED UNFAIRLY

I attended Berkeley High School, which was not the feeder school for my middle school. As a result, I had no friends or relationships when I first arrived. In an effort to have a social outlet I tried out for the varsity wrestling team. I made the team, and I considered this a significant accomplishment.

Cliques form and allegiances emerge within all kinds of teams. When an outsider shows up, they disrupt the norms. In this case, I was a disrupter, an outsider. Coaches at all levels of sports tend to have favorites. If you played a sport and weren't one of those people, you notice. My wrestling coach had favorites and made no effort to conceal it.

When the wrestling season started, it overlapped with the football season. Many players on the football team wanted to join the wrestling team after their season ended. Of course, the wrestling coach wanted these football players on his team too. In order to work around this conundrum, he allowed football players to take spots on the wrestling team without going through tryouts like the rest of the team members, me included. This made it possible for the football players to show up and enter wrestling competitions without even having attended practice. Since I was new, I was unaware of this custom.

Prior to the football season ending, our wrestling team was doing well. We were in first place within our conference. I had competed in six matches and had won all six.

On the day of a wrestling match, each athlete received the team uniform displaying their weight class. Before the seventh match, I went to the athletics window to check out the uniform. The student issuing them informed me that it had been checked out by another student. I was confused by this and thought it was an error. I went to the coach to see what was going on. He informed me that he had given the weight class to someone else, a football player who'd just joined the team after the football season ended. The coach never informed me prior to giving my slot away. At that moment I didn't know how to respond, so I said nothing and walked away.

The team left and went to the match. I was upset over what had happened. I accepted the circumstances, knowing they were unfair. I moved on, not planning to return to the team. The next day, a couple of team members sought me out. They were angry over the process and what had happened. They felt it was wrong. They went on and on about how I had been shafted and shouldn't let it go. They had lost the match. The wrestler who replaced me had lost, causing them to lose by one match. I gave a lot of thought to what they said. I knew it was unfair; however, not being from the school or the area I didn't see many options. The coach was showing favoritism, and that's what coaches do. That was the way I saw it.

The next day I went to practice. When I walked in, I let the coach know that I was there to reclaim my spot on the varsity team.

"I'm not from here and I was not aware of the rules you had. Further, this is a competition, isn't it? Then I'm willing to wrestle for the spot on the team."

The team was watching us, as was the individual who had been given my spot on the team. I walked onto the mat and waited. The wrestler who had been given my spot walked over to me and said, "You can have the spot back."

We did not have to wrestle for it. He knew that I was a strong wrestler and that he could lose. He also knew that what had happened wasn't right. A few team members came over to me and gave me a pat on the back. The coach didn't say a word. I was not from there and, in his mind, had no allegiance to him. I was an outsider who was willing to challenge the custom my way. This is what outsiders can do to a group. He knew, I knew, and the team knew he had failed as a coach. He was allowing an unfair practice. It was a custom, but that didn't make it right.

My experience with the wrestling coach illustrates how showing favoritism will cause any leader to lose respect among the team. You cannot be an effective leader if you have lost the respect of your team. When employees feel there is preferential treatment given to a group or individual, they will resent it.

"Birds of a feather flock together" is a common phrase. When off the job, employees are often friends. They play together in sports leagues, attend church, go to one another's weddings, and hang out after hours. They share their experiences and feelings about work. There are no secrets. Everyone knows when their bosses offer special treatment to their peers. If one of them feels unfairly treated, their entire clique or group will join in the sentiment. When you are a fair leader, word spreads. So does unfairness.

I was assigned to be a manager for a delivery operation early in my career. In an earlier section I discussed meeting the influencers, and I referred to a shop steward. He would know what the primary employee complaints were since he fielded them daily. He let me know that the junior driver's main complaint was that Rich, their supervisor, showed favoritism. Rich had thirty-two drivers in his group and was directly responsible for all aspects of their work. He gave them their work assignments, scheduled their day-off requests, and trained them.

After meeting with the steward and getting the lay of the land, I met with a junior driver to hear the complaint firsthand. I spent the entire day with him while he delivered his route. The first topic he wanted to discuss was *favoritism.*

Over the next three days, I went out with three drivers. All three drivers were bitter about what they believed to be Rich's unfair practices regarding work assignments. As junior drivers, they were typically used as "cover drivers," designated drivers who were called on to cover for employees who were on vacation or taking a sick or personal day.

Rich had discretion to train new drivers on whatever routes he felt they were best suited. Of course, if given a choice, a young driver would prefer delivering to homes along the beach versus a business park. All employees know what the choice assignments are in any business situation. As a supervisor Rich assigned physically smaller male drivers and women to cover the less strenuous positions daily when he could; the junior employees took note. Technically, he was not doing anything incorrect. He had created a custom within the workgroup. It was unspoken, but the nonverbal actions spoke loudly. And naturally, the larger and more physical employees in cover roles resented this.

I took Rich out to lunch to share what I'd learned from my meetings with the junior drivers. After some small talk, I asked him to write down what constitutes being a fair leader. I let him know that I wanted to use his list as a guide so that he and I could be on the same page. The top things on his list were:

- Treating others as you want to be treated.

- Listening to your people.

- Building trust.

- Giving employees advance notice on big changes affecting their job.

The list went on, but these top four were predictable to me. All supervisors know what to do—they just have a problem executing their ideas. Knowing is not always doing.

Anticipating he would say these things, I used his list as a way to open the dialogue. After reading through the list, I, in turn, wrote down some questions to ask him that directly correlated to the top items on his list so that he would have to verbalize his own expectations and gauge his actions against his own values. I asked him:

- How do you want to be treated?
- What constitutes being a good listener?
- How do you build trust?
- If your job were being changed, how would you like to be notified?

When Rich was done answering these, I asked him, "Do you lead in a way that is consistent with your list? Do your employees see you as fair?"

He thought most of his employees believed he was fair but admitted some didn't. In his mind, the route assignments were based on the knowledge employees possessed. If they had been trained in an area, then they would cover those areas. He did not attribute placement to their junior status, gender, or physical prowess.

I placed the list of drivers covering the more scenic, less intense positions on the table in front of him. Next to it I placed the list of drivers in the more physically difficult areas.

"So, tell me why all of the women cover drivers

and physically smaller male drivers are in the less intense areas?"

He hesitated. I could see him attempting to develop a response to support this obvious bias.

Before he answered I asked, "Who decides where drivers are initially trained to cover positions? Who decides where they will gain knowledge?"

"I made those decisions based on future needs," Rich answered.

"Then why, when female drivers or male drivers who are under six feet are hired, are the needs always in the areas deemed the most favorable?" I finally asked.

"I can see how that looks," he responded.

Rich knew what he was doing, and I knew what he was doing. More importantly, his people knew. He wasn't technically breaking any policies or rules. He was applying a discretion, allowed to him at the time, about where he would train cover employees.

"Let's compare your list of what a fair leader looks like to this issue," I suggested.

Rich said we didn't need to do that. He could see the issue. He wanted to place employees on routes he believed to be their best fit. By doing so he felt he couldn't accommodate everyone.

"Rich, your employees all make the same wage essentially. In their minds, they all signed on to do the same job. Yes or no?" I asked.

"Of course."

"Then you decide to change that practice, correct?"

"Yes, but it is based on business needs," Rich said.

"Do you think that they see that as fair, Rich?"

"No," he said.

"So are you in fact a fair leader?"

He struggled with this but begrudgingly agreed and said, "No."

"Fairness, Rich, is not what you think it is; it's what the employees believe it is. When leaders institute their own customs, some employees benefit, but most do not. Their work performance will be impacted by what they see as fair treatment. So you listed treating others as you want to be treated, listening to them, and building trust. These doors do not open in an environment where favoritism is obvious. You assign females and physically smaller drivers to cover beautiful, pristine areas. Is that favoritism?"

His answer was, "Yes, and I will change this."

Rich announced to his group that he would be cross-training the cover driver group more deeply and would prepare for upcoming summer vacations. The first driver he trained was a female driver to cover a route that was in a business park. He continued to train drivers so that all would be used fairly. There was an immediate recognition of the change by the union representatives. They appreciated the more fairly administered approach and let the supervisor know they appreciated it. He told me he had received the praise and he felt good about it. Being fair precludes building trust. You cannot build trust as a leader without this ingredient first.

I often noticed a pattern. When an employee believed they were being treated unfairly, they generally sought help beyond their immediate supervisor. They called an employee hotline, took the issue to the human resources group, or in many cases went to their union representative. I served as the president of five separate business units for UPS, including Chicago, Virginia, and Southern California. In that capacity I wanted all employee complaints that came in through the hotline placed on my desk daily. I reviewed them weekly with the director of human resources, who investigated the situations and managed them accordingly.

I read a complaint once from an employee named Dan, a large man who stood about six feet two and had a gregarious personality. I was familiar with him, and he also happened to work in the facility where my office was located. I knew him to be an excellent employee who was engaged in our employee health and safety committees. His complaint stated that it was wrong for him to be forced to work ten to twelve hours a day when others were working just over eight. Employees who were the managers' favorites and those who were poor performers were getting the smallest and shortest workloads. He had spoken to his manager multiple times yet had gotten nowhere.

I called Sarah, the division manager, and reviewed the complaint with her. She stated she would look into it right away and speak to Dan personally when he arrived for work. On a whim, I asked if I could accompany her so that I could hear what he had to say. Numerous complaints had been coming in about excessive overtime. I wanted to hear it from the horse's mouth without someone filtering the information.

Later, Sarah and I met with Dan's manager, Ron, and reviewed the complaint. Ron expressed his disappointment that the employee had gone over his head.

When Dan arrived for work, Sarah let him know she had his complaint and wanted to review it. He was pleased to see that his complaint had gotten such a quick response. She asked Dan to come into a nearby office with her. I accompanied them. Sarah read the complaint aloud so she could verify it was accurate. Many times, when complaints were phoned in, they were not transcribed correctly. Dan acknowledged that what it stated was accurate.

"How much overtime can you work weekly?" Sarah asked.

"I can work overtime two to three times a week, but right now it's every day. There are others working overtime one, maybe two days a week. I've spoken to Ron, my manager, a few times but nothing changes," Dan said.

"What did Ron say to you when you asked to work less overtime?"

"Ron said he would try to keep it to two to three days a week but that I am a cover employee and as such would work a lot of overtime."

"Are all the cover employees working daily overtime like you?" Sarah asked.

At this point Dan amplified his voice and became agitated.

"No, they are not. Ron takes care of his guys, the ass-kissers, and I am not going to kiss his ass to get less overtime," he said.

I merely observed the discussion and made no comment. Sarah explained she would review the issue with Ron, and the three of them would discuss it the next day. Dan thanked her for looking into it and dismissed himself. After Dan left, Sarah and I discussed what we'd heard.

"Sarah, what do you think the real issue is?" I asked.

"I think Ron is slow to listen and respond to his people at times and their needs," Sarah replied.

"Perhaps that is true, but I see a few things here. Number one: Good work shouldn't turn into more work," I said.

Sarah agreed.

"Additionally," I continued, "Dan feels he is being taken advantage of because he is. He is working twelve hours a day, while employees producing less are being given less hours. That is a formula that fails every time. It creates resentment."

As a UPS business unit president with twenty thousand people working under me, I'd witnessed this behavior countless times and could accurately assess what was really going on.

"Dan's comments on favorites are in fact accurate, because that is what he perceives it to be. He said the ass-kissers are getting less work. His perception rules," I continued.

A couple of days later Sarah came to see me and confirmed that my assessment of the situation was accurate. In Ron's operation, the employees who were the most efficient were getting the most daily work. They were his younger, newer employees—and the ones less likely to rock the boat. The older, more senior employees were getting eight hours of work daily and some were getting fewer.

In this example, we see a few things. The manager was punishing junior employees with overtime they didn't want. This manager created a psychological expectation that junior employees got the most overtime and senior employees would get less overtime. Ron ignored the junior employee complaints because correcting the problem meant adding overtime for senior employees. He was making a choice to favor one group over another. This is a perfect example of favoritism. He assumed the employees would just accept the situation. They did not. This was always the case when I saw employees go over their supervisor's or manager's head.

As a leader you will have blind spots, things about yourself you don't see. Your people will see them. When you have been unfair to an employee, they may not let you know personally. They will, however, develop attitudes and behaviors consistent with being treated unfairly. They may go over your head and complain about work assignments. They may be irritable or short-tempered. There will be signs. There are always signs, but you have to be willing to see them. If you don't want employees going over your head, then you must address their concerns genuinely. Terms and conditions between you and your team surrounding fairness must be established. Then you as their leader must live up to those agreements.

EXERCISES

In your group, identify some practices that are cultural norms, not rules or policies. Are they fair to all people within the group?

Do your employees know it is OK to bring issues to you personally that they see as unfair? If so, what terms and conditions have you established with them to ensure they do so?

Identify your biases surrounding your employees. Who are your favorites? Who are your least favorites?

How will you lead in a way that removes these biases? What will you change?

CHAPTER THREE

PERSONAL ETHICS— DO THE RIGHT THING

....

According to the Emotions in the Workplace Initiative at the Yale Center for Emotional Intelligence, "nearly one in four U.S. workers surveyed say they 'sometimes,' 'often,' or 'almost always' feel pressured to act unethically while on the job."[1]

While working in my grandfather's barbershop, I overheard lots of conversations. In one instance, a man was excitedly telling someone how he had sold his car for three thousand dollars. He explained that the engine was about to fail and needed work, so he had dodged a bullet by selling it to some unsuspecting individual. Both men laughed. My grandfather shook his head while looking at them and said, "What goes around comes around, you know."

---
[1] "The Emotions in the Workplace Initiative at the Yale Center for Emotional Intelligence," *Harvard Business Review*, October 2020.

The man who sold his car had done nothing outside of the law. He had no legal obligation to reveal what he knew about the future repairs the car would need. Therein lies the key aspect of being ethical. It requires having a moral conscience. **As a leader you can be within your rights about a decision you make on an issue and yet be unethical.**

ETHICAL BEHAVIOR: ARE YOU HONORABLE?

Your most valuable possession is your reputation. This applies both to your professional and personal lives. Behave unethically, and your reputation will be directly aligned with your actions. People will never trust you.

Jim Casey, the UPS founder, defined ethical behavior as *honorable conduct toward others.* So what is "honorable conduct"? It is conduct in which you don't deceive or intentionally seek to take advantage of someone. This is true for businesses and for the individuals who lead or manage the business, as they are one and the same.

Companies have a requirement to conduct business fairly and ethically. There are numerous laws and regulations to ensure this happens. Yet there are many examples of unethical businesses where people are taken advantage of. Ethics is a topic that is so complex, it is a requirement for many college degrees. Many businesses have ethics committees. The US Congress has an ethics committee, and so do many city councils. Time after time, you hear about some politician being charged with ethical violations. The same happens in business. In this chapter we will examine our *personal* ethics in our dealings with others.

Ethical violations I've witnessed in the workplace involved deception and a general lack of morality (that is, knowing the difference between right and wrong, and choosing wrong anyway). Almost always, these violations were self-serving in nature. The leader had the ability to deceive someone for personal benefit and did so—not unlike when a used-car salesman sells a car in need of repairs and conceals that information from the buyer. In the workplace it can look like an employee request for a day off that can't be accommodated, but to keep the peace, the manager still says, "I'll try." Since the manager had no intention of granting the employee the day off, these actions were unethical.

JUST BECAUSE IT'S LEGAL DOESN'T MAKE IT ETHICAL

One of the most famous companies that violated business ethics was the energy company Enron. They went bankrupt and cost investors seventy-four billion dollars. Thousands of people lost their jobs, and many, like a friend of mine, even lost their entire life savings. Enron had been using accounting principles that were legal at the time but have since been banned. The leaders of the organization were indicted.

The case took years to resolve because these leaders technically did not break any law, but rather they deceived their investors, thus acting unethically. They knew what they were doing was wrong and could harm others, but they did it anyway. Perhaps they were able to justify their actions to themselves because they could tell themselves their behavior was "legal."

This sounds familiar. We see this happen over and over again in business.

Take opioids, for example. In this drug's illegal form, it's called heroin and other street names. But in the legal and regulated world of Big Pharma, opioids include a large slate of pain-killing drugs. Oxycodone, morphine, and Percocet are just a few.

These drugs are cited as being responsible for over one hundred thousand deaths annually in the United States. Selling drugs such as oxycodone is legal, and doctors prescribe them as painkillers. However, Big Pharma deceived doctors and the public about the drugs' efficacy and how addictive they are. This led to widespread chemical dependency on legal drugs and at the same time increased demand. Doctors, incentivized to keep prescribing, did so, even as more people grew dependent. A full-blown opioid epidemic emerged, with millions of people addicted.

Since these tactics were discovered, multiple states and municipalities that bear the weight of addiction, crime, and subsequent poverty have successfully sued the pharmaceutical companies that produce and distribute these drugs. In February 2022, a national settlement was reached with some of the violating companies, totaling twenty-six billion dollars. These funds will go to thousands of US communities that successfully proved the companies knowingly deceived the public and hence acted unethically. Companies knew they were lying while they were raking in the profits. Doctors were also making millions by overprescribing these pills, particularly in poor communities. The states and cities took the position that the providers knowingly supported this practice for financial gain. By doing so they harmed the community and destroyed millions of lives.

This case has taken over ten years to resolve. The companies defended their actions, citing that no legal violations had occurred, which was true. Ultimately, the case was viewed through an ethical lens. The companies did, in fact, violate the code of ethics around doing business with the medical community. Physicians swear to the Hippocratic oath, requiring them to be ethical to all whom they serve. In this case the courts agreed that they were encouraged by these companies to be unethical. The physicians and the companies were both punished. Physicians who were involved have been criminally prosecuted as well. They were all unethical and all paid the price.

Leaders, like companies, are expected to be ethical in their personal dealings. Once your ethics are deemed questionable, your ability to lead others will diminish and possibly end. I've seen many good leaders fail or lose their jobs because of a decision they made or action they took that, after investigation, was deemed unethical.

Another area related to ethics is health and safety requirements within organizations, which have evolved significantly over the last thirty years. Companies today are expected to put their employees' personal safety above all else while doing business. That was not the case in the 1980s and '90s. I know because I witnessed the change. In those decades, companies allowed employees to adhere loosely to safety requirements if it meant getting the job done. If an employee was driving a vehicle, staying at the speed limit was required only if it did not interfere with getting there on time.

Highway accidents involving long-haul drivers became a particular focus in the 1980s. This was due to the increase in fatal accidents involving this group. According to the Federal Motor Carrier Safety Administration, from 1975 to 1980 fatal crashes grew from 4,304 to 6,431. This made 1980 the highest level on record. Many of these drivers worked independently and transported heavy loads such as vehicles, gasoline, chemicals, and everything you can imagine. They were paid by the mile with incentives for beating schedules. Their goals were to drive as many miles as possible, as quickly as possible. The incentives encouraged driving well beyond human endurance limits—namely, those needed for proper sleep and health. Falling asleep behind the wheel was common. The results could be catastrophic. Rules and regulations mattered until they got in the way of doing the job quickly. The companies and leaders knew their employees were beating schedules only because drivers were defying the legal speed limits and weren't getting enough sleep. Many of these companies were included in lawsuits where accidents and fatalities occurred. It was unethical for the companies not to question or stop behaviors they knew to be a risk to the public.

The Occupational Safety and Health Administration (OSHA) is the federal agency charged with protecting the public and ensuring that safety is not disregarded. In the late 1980s, they began conducting random visits to companies to ensure regulations were being adhered to.

Many years ago, when I was the president of a unit, one of my operations received a surprise visit from an OSHA representative to perform an audit. The auditor's role is to ensure that all OSHA guidelines regarding a safe workplace are in effect. He went through the facility and inspected the equipment for legal compliance. The equipment and all systems passed with flying colors. The auditor then reviewed all employees' training records. The records were in order; all the training requirements had been completed.

The final step of the audit involved interviewing employees. During the interviews, the auditor's task was to verify that the training was, in fact, successfully retained and that the employee was using the skills. While completing this portion of the audit, the auditor discovered that numerous employees had signed their certification forms the prior day. In his final report the auditor made a note of this as being suspicious. This was *technically* not a violation, as OSHA only required to have the certifications on file, which they were.

When an employee is hired in any company there are requirements to train them on the safety protocols *before* they start working. How to exit in case of an emergency, for example, is a simple protocol, yet it saves lives. In the operation I am discussing, that was not done. We required any employee to complete the safety training prior to starting work, on day one, not day five, no exception. Yet the manager of the operation that was audited had not done this properly. Both he and the human resources manager knew it did not occur. The audit reflected the company's lack of follow-through on this issue.

Once the human resource manager reviewed the audit information, he could have accepted the results and said, "Great—no violations." To his credit, he did not. There had been a clear ethical violation. He accepted responsibility for what had happened.

The manager of the operation was interviewed and admitted that he'd had his supervisors complete the safety certifications the day before the audit. He had heard some chatter about a possible visit from OSHA. In his effort to be compliant he made sure all the documentation was filed to the letter. However, the manager had failed to properly train his people when they were first hired in a way that would ultimately protect them. What is more important: a signed document or ensuring employee safety from the outset? Completing the certifications the day before the audit provided the illusion that he was keeping up with company standards and was concerned for his employees' safety. This was false. If he truly cared about his employees, he would have trained them right away.

The manager rationalized that he was missing a number of supervisors, so he and his team were spread very thin. He had eliminated a number of administrative activities temporarily that he saw as nonessential when it came to getting the job done. In his mind, he was prioritizing customers and the company's commitment to them. He compromised his ethics when he asked the supervisors to hastily fill out the paperwork, and they supported his deception.

The manager was demoted to a position of lesser responsibility as a consequence of his action. His team retained their positions yet also suffered consequences. They received no pay increases that year. Their reputations were also tainted, a far more severe punishment.

In many ways, the manager got off easy. He was lucky no was injured or worse because of his unethical actions.

Over the course of my career, I have witnessed many people get into similar situations. The manager's first ethical mistake was taking a shortcut. Shortcuts can work when they are on your computer, but they do not work in business.

ETHICS ARE ABOUT DOING THE RIGHT THING ALL THE TIME.

Successful leaders are ethical. Procedures are put in place for a reason. Ethical leaders follow them not because they are a rule but because they are morally right.

PERSONAL ETHICS: THE BUCK STOPS WITH *YOU*

Ethical behavior is a self-policing value that leaders should uphold and demonstrate. You will see people behave unethically around you. You cannot control the morals and values of others. Being ethical requires a moral compass. Unfortunately, not every person has one.

YOUR PERSONAL ETHICS BELONG TO ONE PERSON: YOU.

When I witnessed a leader receive punishment for violating ethics, they often tried to defend themselves by explaining that their bosses made them do it. That never worked.

THE ONE THING YOU GET TO CONTROL 100 PERCENT OF THE TIME IS YOUR OWN BEHAVIOR.

Holding employees accountable to established company standards is one of the roles of leadership. Yet many leaders fail to do this, and it always catches up to them. Companies may have standards that include dealing with conflict, discussing work performance, and ensuring employees are dependable.

One example from my career involved new supervisors who compromised their ethics when it came to employee attendance. When employees are hired, they know they are expected to be reliable. Their supervisors are expected to hold them to that standard. However, when employees miss work or are late to work excessively and the issue is not addressed, a pattern develops.

The supervisors ignored the issue until they were questioned by upper management about why they had such a staffing problem. Closer examination demonstrated the departments didn't lack staff. Rather, there was an employee attendance issue. The supervisors increased their efforts by focusing on attendance and began using mass discipline to correct the pattern. They threatened the employees: "If you don't come to work reliably, you'll be terminated." Attendance improved for a brief period, then fell back, because no one initially addressed the real issue: What is the honorable/right thing to do?

Dennis, a manager, had a chronic attendance problem within his operation. Dennis had five lead supervisors who led thirty-two other supervisors with approximately five hundred employees under them. The operation had a staffing plan that allowed 15 percent of his employees to be out daily. This would permit all employee entitlements to be covered while providing the necessary levels of employees needed daily. Over 25 percent of Dennis's employees were absent daily. This meant that he was operating with fifty fewer employees than his operation needed. This resulted in the operation running late daily, thereby creating service delays for the customers. When Dennis learned the problem was up for review, he demonstrated typical behavior: He had each of his lead supervisors prepare a presentation to show what steps they were taking to improve attendance rates.

A review with the division manager was scheduled and I attended. Dennis had one of his supervisors open with a presentation. They each began by stating that they had gone through all employee attendance records and were issuing disciplinary notifications to any employee who had missed work beyond company standards. After seeing the first two identical presentations, I stopped them and asked if we could have a roundtable conversation.

I opened the discussion by asking the group, "I would like all of you to hand me the records of the employees who have had stellar attendance." The supervisors became visibly uncomfortable, and they handed them to me. I looked at the area on the records where the supervisors could make comments on any discussions they'd had with the person. These were the excellent employees and there were no comments on attendance. In fact, there were no comments of any kind.

I then asked them to hand me the records for those who were chronically absent or late. As I suspected, there were no comments of any kind on those either. This indicated that the employees working for this group were not getting any developmental feedback, good or bad.

"Who sets the standards for the employees

daily?" I asked the group.

"We do," they all answered.

"For your employees who are reliable and dependable daily, what comments or recognition have you given them?" I asked.

The supervisors were silent. Each one had a puzzled expression.

"The same comments we have for our unreliable employees," Dennis interjected.

"That's correct, Dennis. If good attendance receives the same recognition as poor attendance, what is the benefit of being reliable?" I asked.

"There isn't any benefit?" one of the supervisors responded.

"So, what will you change?" I asked.

Dennis responded that he needed to have his group of supervisors develop a process that would recognize those who were consistently reliable.

"I would like you all to realize that positive behavior that is recognized gets repeated," I added.

I suggested that employee recognition should be conducted weekly for all employees with good records. Consistency was important. This recognition should be given in front of their peers. Being reliable had not mattered in the past. This would set a term and condition with their group that it did matter. Unreliable employees would see this recognition and know that it mattered. There would be no surprise when their lack of attendance or behavior was addressed. The division manager offered his support in assisting them with these efforts.

Finally, I asked the supervisors to give me their definition of ethics. Answers included having integrity, being moral, and treating others as you wished to be treated. I asked them to google the definition and then asked one of the supervisors to read it aloud to the group.

He read: "Moral principles that govern a person's behavior."

"As leaders we always have an obligation to be honorable toward those we lead. In looking at the records of your employees, I saw no comments about attendance, good or bad, on them. Yet you are going to take discipline on employees you have never forewarned. Is that ethical?"

"No, it is not," they all agreed.

I restated to the group that they could be technically right in a decision they make, such as giving disciplinary warnings, yet still be unethical. They are the ones who changed the terms and conditions of the requirements for reliable attendance. They misled their employees. They were allowed to be late and absent with no discussions or warnings of consequences. They just did what the supervisors allowed. However, when the leaders were called out for it, they began blaming their employees and threatening their jobs. That is deceptive and morally wrong; it is unethical.

"So what is important here? Protecting your ethics and doing the right thing or disciplining your people unfairly?" I asked.

Of course, they agreed that protecting their ethics was more important. In college settings, topics such as politically driven ethics or the actions of those in the business arena take up the majority of the discussion. Personal actions in the workplace between the leader and their employees are rarely discussed. The workplace is where you live and lead. Ethical issues in this arena are just more complex.

You are the ethical conscience within your team. Your role is not only to display ethical behavior but also to prevent unethical behaviors. To be ethical you must always have morals and do the right thing.

EXERCISES

In each case, what would ethical leadership look like?

- You have some employees who wear athletic shoes occasionally to work. The job requires work boots for reasons of safety, but you have let this slide. An order comes down that all employees wearing improper footwear are not to be allowed to work. A number of employees continue to come to work in athletic footwear.

- You get a new female employee, and male employees begin to ask her out and harass her repeatedly with comments. She just wants to do her job and fit in.

- You have an employee who is fast at the job yet cuts corners to accomplish this. He is risking his safety, but this employee hates being corrected and slows his productivity when you correct him.

- You get a new employee but your boss requests that you bypass the prework orientation training and start them immediately.

CHAPTER FOUR

LISTENING— A SKILL OR A VALUE?

EMPLOYEES DO NOT always like one another or get along. Today, that is true more than ever. There are many lightning rod issues, such as the approach to the pandemic, divided politics, the war in Gaza, and the situation in Ukraine. These issues can drive divisions in your team's relationships with you and with one another. Employees bring all of their beliefs with them to work. Disagreements and even harassment among members of the team have always been components of the workplace. This is not new.

As the leader, what and who you listen to will be impacted by your personal values. Negative feelings about an employee will prevent you from listening to them if you allow it. As the leader, you cannot allow it. The catchphrase "I'm only human" is generally used when being emotional has driven a bad decision. That doesn't work when you are in a leadership role. After I had made an emotionally driven (and bad) decision, one of my mentors told me, "The biggest barrier you will face as a leader will be that you are human. So, Noel, you don't get to be human."

You cannot allow your likes and dislikes to rule your judgments as a leader or to prevent you from truly listening.

EMPATHETIC LISTENING

Empathetic listening is the practice of being attentive and responsive to others' input during conversations. When you listen empathetically you don't just hear someone's words—you feel their emotional state. During chaotic times as a leader, you may fail to hear the signs your employees are giving you. When you're driving your car and you hit something in the road and hear a loud bang, you take the off-ramp and inspect the vehicle to see if there is damage. This same thing applies when a troubled employee is speaking to you. Get off the road and pay attention.

If you don't, it can lead to bad outcomes. Empathetic listening can only be done when you intentionally pause and evaluate the situation.

WHY IT PAYS TO LISTEN EMPATHETICALLY

The following is a great example of why the value of listening is critical to effective leadership.

In 2006 we had two employees who had an altercation that turned physical. Typically, the employee committing the violent act is terminated. However, there are many levels of potential liability that can follow a workplace violence incident. Charges can be filed with the police by the employee who's been struck. Civil lawsuits can be filed against the employee who committed the violence. The company can be sued. Even after an employee is fired, an investigation into the incident ensues.

I received a call from the manager the two employees worked for, informing me of the situation. When an employee commits an act of violence, security escorts them out of the facility; in very serious situations the police are called. As for the penalty, that is not determined until a hearing is held.

The manager explained that Joe, twenty-eight years old, had so aggressively pushed Rick, forty-six, that Rick fell. More than a dozen employees witnessed the incident. Joe had been in his position for a few months. Rick had twenty-five years on the job. The manager stated that he would investigate what happened and include the human resources manager in the process and update me on his findings once they were complete.

The manager called back a short while later and reviewed what he knew of the facts of the incident. He started by saying that Rick, the older employee, was excellent at his job. There had never been a problem or any concerns with him. Joe, the newer employee, was not doing well in his position and was a loner. The morning of the incident, some employees saw the two of them talking, when suddenly Joe pushed Rick, who fell down hard as a result. It seemed straightforward to the manager: The workplace code of conduct had been violated. He would pursue full termination of Joe. I let that stand and did not ask any questions. My morning was very hectic, and I had other things to get to. I thanked the manager for the update.

The next morning Tom, a representative of the local union, called me to discuss the incident between Rick and Joe. It was common for local union leaders to attempt to go over the head of those responsible for handling employee-management relations, known as the labor managers. They wanted to go right to the top when they had an issue. I wasn't going to allow that. I let Tom know that any concerns he had could be taken to Mark, the director of labor relations, and there was nothing for us to discuss. Joe had struck Rick in the workplace, and we would not tolerate that behavior. This was an open-and-shut case, as far as I was concerned. In my mind, there was nothing more to listen to. Tom told me he was very disturbed by my answer and hung up.

Mark later called to tell me he'd just gotten a call from Tom. Tom was very upset because I would not listen to what he had to say. I told Mark that he was correct—I would not discuss the termination with Tom. I let Tom know that if he wanted to discuss it, he needed to talk with Mark. Mark explained there was more to the incident than even he knew and felt

I should be aware. He said, "Noel, I know you like to hear it from the horse's mouth. I'll have Tom call you again. I would like you to listen to him. It will save me some time when we talk again."

I agreed to schedule an in-person meeting with Tom, as opposed to a call, and promised I would do a follow-up with him.

Tom came to my office the next day. I had arranged a meeting between the two of us. I apologized for the misunderstanding the previous day. I let him know I believed he was attempting to cut Mark out of the process, and I could not allow the overstepping of the labor manager. Tom said he understood; however, he felt that this situation was unusual. He then went on to review with me some factors that he had discovered during his investigation as the union representative. When he began to speak, I took out a notepad. Whenever I need to listen empathetically, I tell myself: **Stop-Pause-Listen** (more on this strategy soon). This always sets the tone for me. I then tune in and listen closely.

Tom began explaining that Rick had been hazing Joe. This had gone on from the first day Joe started. Rick had a personal issue with Joe's uncle.

Rick and his wife had divorced two years previously, and she'd married Joe's uncle. Rick hurled insults at Joe daily, specifically degrading the uncle and Rick's ex-wife. The last straw was when Rick said to Joe, "Your new aunt is a whore, your mother is a whore, and your entire family are whores." That was when Joe pushed him, causing him to fall.

This changed things. I asked Tom if management was aware of Rick's daily harassment of Joe. He said yes, the manager had been asked repeatedly to address the issue and to stop it, and he had not. Tom said that as bad as the situation was, there was a lot of guilt on the part of others. In his view, if the manager had done his job, the altercation would never have occurred. Tom added that he was opposed to Joe being terminated. He felt a suspension was in order, along with reassignment to a different workgroup. He was speaking to me because he knew I would have to support such an outcome. I made no agreements. I said I would talk to Mark, and he would get back to Tom. I asked a few follow-up questions, and we ended the session.

When Mark spoke to the manager, he admitted that Joe had asked him to get the harassment to stop.

He also said that newer employees always get hazed a bit and he assumed that was all that was happening. He had mentioned to Rick that he should lighten up some. Mark asked Rick if his manager had asked him to stop the harassment, and Rick said no. Mark then asked Rick if he had made the comments about Joe's family; he denied saying those things. Though witnesses saw the push, none would admit to hearing what had been said, so it could not be proven.

Not surprisingly Joe filed a civil lawsuit, and Rick filed an assault charge. The company and the union had to hire attorneys. The result? Joe got his job back, and the company was ordered to pay out over seventy thousand dollars in back pay, since he lost a year of work while the case was being resolved. Additionally, the organization had to pay over two hundred thousand dollars in attorney's fees. It's safe to say that all of this could have easily been avoided if the manager listened to the employee he didn't value.

When the manager reported the incident to me, he had given some clues about his true feelings. He explained that the older employee was "excellent." With that statement he clearly communicated a bias. He didn't recognize this because he was not listening empathetically. He said the younger employee was a loner and not doing well at his job—again, a bias. He never mentioned the harassment the younger employee had asked him to stop. He blew it off, and his actions supported this. The manager clearly demonstrated a bias for Rick over Joe. This manager was reprimanded for his failure to stop the harassment. So in examining this scenario, we see:

- The manager had a positive bias toward Rick; therefore, he did not listen empathetically to Joe's frustration. The manager didn't value Joe and did not give his respect and attention to him.

- I listened empathetically to Mark, the labor relations manager, because I *valued* his input, and I respected him. When he asked me to meet with Tom, I agreed.

- The implications of the manager's actions led to a civil court case. Hundreds of thousands of dollars were lost.

- The manager was reprimanded for his actions.

The most effective way to gather information is to *listen actively and empathetically* to what is being said. You may *hear* someone talking, but that is not listening. Listening to a podcast is a popular way to learn, for example. I listen to quite a few podcasts. The ones I enjoy the most teach me something. The same holds true for seminars. When I attend one, I am looking to learn something, so I listen closely to the speaker. Occasionally, I take notes. I often think of the old saying, "What you see, you remember. What you hear, you forget. What you do, you know." So I often take notes while listening and write down things I want to know. I don't just listen. I write the key points down. According to writer Elyse Hauser, we retain the information we write down 97 percent better than simply listening.[1]

    Critical listening is a developed skill. However, before you listen to anything or anyone intentionally, you must value the person or the topic. You must respect the speaker providing the information. Respecting others by listening attentively is a reflection of our values. Interrupting people while they speak is rude; finishing their sentences for them is inconsiderate. We don't do these things to people whose input we *value*.

---

[1] Elyse Hauser, "Here's Why You Remember Things Better When You Write Them Down," LifeSavvy, March 2020.

STOP-PAUSE-LISTEN: VALUING YOUR SPEAKER

As a leader you will face challenges if you don't already possess a personal value aligned with listening to your people. This is particularly true regarding people with whom you don't have a strong relationship or people you simply don't value. Our personal feelings cannot be allowed to impede how well we listen to someone. This is not to say that you must agree with everything your people say or that you must do everything they want. But you do have an obligation as their leader to allow them to express their views, problems, concerns, and feelings.

Your ability to listen to someone will be influenced by factors such as:

- Do you respect them as a person, which leads to respecting what they have to say?

- Do you value their experience?

- Do you have openness to views that differ from your own?

- Does your ego interfere with solutions being offered that you did not create?

- Do you allow task-related busywork to be more important than listening to an employee?

These are some typical factors to consider when determining whether your personal values reflect the importance of listening consistently to others and identifying personal barriers you may face in putting that value into practice. If you don't have openness to views that are different from your own, for example, that may become a barrier to effective listening.

Even if you do your best, everyone can face environmental barriers to deep listening.

The day-to-day challenges of being a leader and juggling multiple priorities while having a group of people pass information to you will be daunting. The biggest obstacle I erected for myself in the beginning of my career, and occasionally at other points, was not truly listening. I did all the normal things that happen when you are in the operation: making decisions, giving out daily work assignments, delivering simple messages, and reporting information to my superiors. *These activities do not require listening—they require talking.* When an employee wants to talk about an issue or has a problem, they don't want you to talk while they communicate. So you can't merely hear them—you have to actively listen. I became a solid listener over time. When someone indicated they wanted to talk, I would use this phrase in my head: **Stop-Pause-Listen.**

So how does "Stop-Pause-Listen" work? It helps to set the stage for fully listening.

- **Stop:** Whatever you are doing, discontinue doing it. No cell phone—do not allow distractions. Focus your attention on the person and nothing else.

- **Pause:** Resist the natural inclination to speak. Do not make assumptions or lead the conversation. Let the person to whom you are listening take the lead. When someone says, "Do you have a moment?" or "I'd like to speak with you," pausing first helps you focus on their state of mind as well as assess their mood, tone, and the challenge they may be facing. You can listen and observe if they are angry, confused, or anxious.

- **Listen:** Let them have the space they need to fully share their issue and feelings. Do not interrupt. Only ask questions to confirm that you fully understand what they are communicating.

A few years ago, I sat through a review of a complaint made by a female employee. The review included the director of human resources, a representative of an agency engaged in employee protections, and me. The representative reviewed the complaint. The employee had reported that she worked in a hostile environment. She was one of four women in a group of forty employees. She was married and had two children and she was receiving daily unwanted advances from her male peers. The harassment from male employees had become too much to bear. She wanted to be able to come to work and just do her job. The representative said she had tears in her eyes while she spoke.

The human resources manager, manager of the operation, and I met to discuss the complaint. The human resources manager opened the meeting stating there was a complaint, and he named the employee. The manager rolled his eyes and said those four—meaning the women—were always complaining about something. The eye-rolling was a sign. I knew immediately that the manager was biased against the women in his charge. The human resources manager reviewed the complaint, which mentioned a supervisor who was one of his direct reports. The employee said she had attempted numerous times to report the harassment to the manager personally. She had spoken with her supervisor multiple times. She had approached the manager and he asked her to make an appointment. Each time she'd tried to make an appointment, he was too busy to speak to her. She'd made two appointments and he'd broken both of them.

While the human resources manager read and reviewed the complaint, I could see the manager physically sinking in his chair. He knew that the employee had tried, and he knew he did not give her the time. He didn't *value* her, and he did not Stop-Pause-Listen. At that moment he was probably wishing he had.

A mistake that many leaders and even companies make is signaling to the employee that they are not important enough to be heard. The consequences for not listening with an open mind can be dire.

Amazon is one of the largest employers in America, with over 1.1 million employees. They have revolutionized the world of e-commerce and will go down in history as one of the greatest organizations of all time. They have been a nonunion employer since they were founded in 1994. It was big news when it was announced in January 2023 that the Amazon employees in Staten Island, New York, took a vote whether to start a union. *Business Insider* reported that the company held over twenty-five anti-union meetings before the voting took place. Companies typically resist having unions represent the employees who work for them. The reasons are varied, but the main reason is that the company loses some degree of control. Without a union, a company's one advantage for that company is it can make changes in operations without negotiating them. This provides agility in serving their customer's needs. With a union they must negotiate changes that affect their workers directly, including wages. I spent my career working with unions, and I understand the need to work with them well.

The person who led the effort was former Amazon employee Chris Smalls. Smalls gave an interview on CNBC after the employees voted for a union. He said he was motivated to organize the employees in this warehouse because Amazon management had been "not listening" to the employees' concerns and complaints for years. The tipping point was the working conditions during COVID. Smalls repeatedly stated in various interviews why he sought to form a union: Amazon, in his view, had dismissed employee concerns and wouldn't provide them with the proper protection. Numerous employees had approached management with other concerns about their well-being. He did not mention these in his interviews, only stating that Amazon management would not listen to any of their concerns. Whether this is true or not is not the point. This is the sentiment Smalls felt and expressed. As a supervisor you are the difference between an employee feeling valued or not as you are the voice of the company. The consequences of employees not feeling heard can be massive. In the case of Amazon, it could cost them billions of dollars.

The position I was charged with upholding during my career was stated in the UPS Policy Book:

"We respond to employee complaints with prompt, sincere attention. Even minor misunderstandings can become major dissatisfaction if overlooked or neglected. When a question exists, we give the employee the benefit of the doubt."

Giving an employee the benefit of the doubt requires taking your ego out of the equation. It requires listening to the employees' words and emotions.

You must pay attention in a way that communicates to the employee: "You are important, and what you have to say matters."

This elevates a person's self-esteem, and they feel valued and heard. When an employee can see that you as the leader value them, they will value and listen to you too.

EXERCISES

On a notepad, write down your responses to these questions.

- Think of a situation where an employee wanted to speak to you one-on-one and you did not give them the time. What were the reasons? What were the results? How will you change your future approach?

- When an employee indicates spontaneously in the future that they want to speak to you, how will you stop? What does this imply? How will you pause? How will you demonstrate to the employee that you are listening? What actions will you take?

- What are the consequences of not listening empathetically? List some of them.

- How is listening a value versus a skill?

CHAPTER FIVE

INTEGRITY—YOUR CROWN JEWEL

In the January 9, 2018, issue of *Inc.* magazine Warren Buffett, one of the wealthiest men in the world, explained what he looked for in people he hired. He said, "You're looking for three things, generally, in a person: Intelligence, energy, and integrity. And if they don't have the last one, don't even bother with the first two."[1]

The crown jewel of the value equation is integrity. The Crown Jewels in England are protected twenty-four hours a day, seven days a week. They are considered the most valuable set of jewels in the world. There has been only one attempt to steal them; they are that secure. Throughout your career, there will be more than one thief who will try to steal your

---

[1] Marcel Schwantes, "Warren Buffett Says If You Hire People on Intelligence but They Lack This Other Trait, Don't Bother," *Inc.*, January 9, 2018.

crown jewel, your integrity. As a leader, you must protect it twenty-four hours a day, seven days a week.

Integrity is defined as "the quality of being honest and having strong moral principles."[2] While I agree with this definition, I don't think it goes far enough. In addition to being honest and moral, it is the strength to keep your word, to do what you say you are going to do, and to be worthy of someone's trust.

On June 24, 2021, a twelve-story condominium in the Miami, Florida, suburb of Surfside collapsed. It happened at 1:22 a.m., while people were in their homes asleep. Ninety-eight people died, and dozens of others were injured and hospitalized. These individuals trusted the structural *integrity* of the building. It failed them.

On August 1, 2007, in Minneapolis, Minnesota, the I-35W bridge was loaded with rush-hour traffic when it collapsed. There were 111 vehicles on it at the time; they all fell into the river below. Thirteen people died and 145 were injured. The drivers trusted the structural *integrity* of the bridge. I am sure they would not have driven on it otherwise.

---

[2] "Integrity," *Cambridge Dictionary Online*, Cambridge University Press, https://dictionary.cambridge.org/us/dictionary/english/integrity.

On October 17, 1989, the Loma Prieta earthquake occurred in the San Francisco Bay Area. There is a portion of expressway that leads from Oakland to San Francisco, known as the Cypress connector, that is of the double-deck variety. The upper section fell onto the lower section, killing forty-two people in the cars below. Earthquakes are common in Northern California, so the expressways are made to withstand them. I used to drive to work daily on this structure. I trusted the *integrity* of it, as did those who were killed.

In all three examples described above, an investigation concluded that the structures had been routinely inspected in accordance with the legal requirements. Engineers had signed documents saying the structures were secure when they were not. Lawsuits followed, and the integrity of those responsible went on trial, not the structures.

Integrity holds everything together, whether a bridge, business, or person. When it fails, everything collapses.

Structural integrity within a team comes from their leader. You are the bridge. I saw many leaders lose their reputations over a lack of integrity. The moment arrived when they needed to be strong to withstand difficulties and the pressures placed on them, and they collapsed. They lost their jobs and careers, as did many of those around them.

The terms and conditions of being a leader require that you have integrity at all times, no matter what. When leaders lose their integrity, there is no recovering from that loss. Their standing with the team and company dies.

Integrity involves the personal commitment you make to yourself to doing what is right and moral at all times—being strong in the face of adversity, keeping your word, and never collapsing.

INTEGRITY: A CORE VALUE

Some years ago, my friend Russell was faced with a situation at work and sought my counsel. When he asked if we could meet for coffee, I sensed some anxiety in his voice. The beginning of the discussion was filled with questions about how my company—where I'd been employed for twenty-three years at that point—handled sales reporting. I was proud of how our sales reporting was managed and explained

INTEGRITY—YOUR CROWN JEWEL

our system. We were known for our integrity and transparency. I told Russell, "The greatest thing about where I've worked is that integrity was a core value of the founder, Jim Casey. He embedded it as a value from the very beginning." Integrity was never a negotiable value for us.

Russell was a salesperson for a large, reputable company that sold construction equipment such as the cranes that you see operating above skyscrapers. These machines could cost millions of dollars. He would see clients and attempt to make a sale. If he succeeded, they would put in an order.

Since Russell hadn't met his sales goals, he was under pressure. His boss suggested that he start reporting promised orders and commitments for that quarter as though those items had been sold. The company policy, however, was that no sale should be counted until a contract was signed. If Russell did what his boss suggested, it would inflate his boss's results for how much the team had sold that quarter.

This request was unethical. Why? To put it plainly, Russell's boss wanted him to falsify his results: to lie, to cheat the system, to give up his integrity. The boss didn't specifically tell Russell to lie—he implied it. Russell immediately became uncomfortable with his boss's suggestion.

"Did anyone hear him suggest this to you?" I asked.

"No," Russell responded.

"There is a reason for that, Russell. Your boss knew it was wrong. It would be your word against his if you took his suggestion and were called out for it. I have seen many people lose their jobs over integrity violations; not once did I hear anyone say it was worth it. I also never witnessed bosses take responsibility for integrity violations by their people."

My advice to Russell was simple: Ask your boss if there is a new policy supporting his suggestion and, if so, request to see it in writing. Do this professionally and with courtesy. Ask your peers if they are getting the same suggestion and if it is a new policy.

The bottom line is this: If you do something you aren't sure is a procedure or policy, only one person will own that. *You!* So get others in the boat with you, and ask for clarification. Don't give your integrity away. You'll never get it back. If it doesn't feel right, it isn't right, so don't do it and don't go it alone.

Two days later Russell called me and thanked me for the advice. He'd asked his boss to see the policy change about reporting sales results. His boss recanted and told him to wait until a contract was in hand before claiming the sale. Russell's actions let his boss know that he wouldn't blindly operate outside company policy. Russell displayed his integrity.

Integrity violations that I witnessed or had to take action against have included falsifying reports, cheating on expense reimbursements, and lying. These individuals violated a policy or broke a law. When these infractions were discovered, they generally resulted in penalties and often termination.

Not all acts where there is a loss of integrity are as obvious as the suggestion Russell got from his boss. In fact, most are more subtle. You can be easily pulled into someone else's integrity violations. This can happen when trust is given and broken between individuals.

Years ago, I knew an individual—let's call him Roy—who worked for a company that issued company credit cards. These cards were, of course, to be used for company business matters. The company did allow for small personal purchases under fifty dollars, such as fuel and food, to be placed on the card. This flexibility was a privilege. When an employee charged personal expenses on the card, he or she was expected to pay them in full each billing cycle.

Roy was running for a political office, to be the representative in his neighborhood. He used his card to purchase fliers and campaign materials, a large expense. He had friends within the company who helped him on his campaign. This was entirely a private pursuit that was being done apart from the job, so there was no issue with his friends helping him. But using the company card for this endeavor violated numerous policies. He was aware of the policies yet ignored them. There are strict laws on the use of any company's funds to support a political campaign. Roy's opponents could claim that his company was funding his campaign, which is clearly illegal.

When the company found out about the charges, they investigated Roy and all the coworkers who had helped him. Roy was terminated for his actions. Those who were helping did not violate any company policies. However, their integrity was called into question. What did they know? If they knew, why didn't they report it? Having integrity supersedes your own personal actions. You must also look out for the individuals around you and understand how they could get into trouble. Roy's coworkers suffered a reputation loss as a result of his actions.

DAY-TO-DAY INTERACTIONS WHERE YOUR INTEGRITY IS AT RISK

Day-to-day interactions with your team will put your personal integrity on full display. In the eyes of your people, even simple situations can be perceived as a lack of integrity. Some common examples are:

- An employee is missing money from their paycheck. They ask you to follow up. You are pulled in many directions that day and forget. The employee asks about the check's status later in the day. Instead of admitting your error, you tell them you haven't heard back from management yet. That is a falsehood. You just lied. It's a trivial lie, no big deal, you tell yourself. Wrong. You violated your integrity to save face with an employee.

- Your manager requests that you put a day-one, newly hired employee to work prior to all of the required certifications being complete.

- You have been informed that some new job assignments are being created and will soon be posted. The employees are not aware of this. Those who apply first will be given priority. You share the information with your favorite employees but withhold it from other employees. This action lacks integrity because you are willfully withholding information and creating an unfair advantage.

- You notice that a peer has been claiming extra mileage on his expense reports. He is stealing, and now you are aware of it. But you don't do or say anything about him committing this act. If you let it be, you are giving away your integrity. You are as guilty as he is because you are complicit.

So how do you protect your integrity? You must commit to being honest and forthright even when faced with adversity. Maintaining integrity requires being stronger than the moment and adhering to moral principles. Integrity is a personal value. Only

INTEGRITY—YOUR CROWN JEWEL

you can personally address barriers or attempts by others to cause a lapse in your integrity. In each instance listed above, there were actions that could have been taken and words that could have been said to reflect your integrity.

I have witnessed all of the examples I listed, and hundreds more. When facing a situation where your integrity is called into question, here are some simple yet powerful statements that can help you defend it.

Scenario 1: You are asked to do something you feel uncomfortable with.

Response to the requester: "I am not comfortable with that request." Or ask questions: "Is that a policy? If so, may I see it? Unless it's a written policy I am not going to do it."

Scenario 2: An employee asks you to keep a policy violation to yourself.

Response to the employee: "I cannot support that request. Either you can report the violation, or I will. However, I will act on it appropriately."

Scenario 3: A piece of equipment needs service because it works inconsistently. There is a safety risk if it is used, yet it is scheduled to be used. Your manager says to use it and not to worry about it.

Response to your manager: "I am not comfortable allowing one of my people to use that piece of equipment, and I won't support its use."

In all of these situations, get others in the boat with you. Don't go it alone. If there is any question, then there is no question. You know what you need to do: Be transparent and ask someone for help. If your company has an employee helpline, you can report the incident there.

COMMUNICATING YOUR INTEGRITY MATTERS!

Paul Fovel, the manager who promoted me to a supervisor position in 1980, provided me with the greatest coaching advice I received during the beginning of my career. He said, "Noel, you are a straight shooter. It's a trait you have that I like the most. You will have a great career if you just keep the work ethic I have seen and you never compromise your integrity. Before I promote you, I want you to look me in the eye and tell me now that you will never compromise your integrity."

I did exactly that. I looked him directly in his eyes and said, "I will never give my integrity away."

And I never did.

I experienced many natural disasters in my career while leading—fires, earthquakes, hurricanes, blizzards, and floods, to name a few. When these situations arose, it was important for me to vocalize the expectation that everyone would follow the rules to the letter. Natural disasters bring their own challenges to getting the job done; they increase stress levels, which impact decision-making. Saying to everyone that no one was to compromise any of our policies or protocols, especially someone's safety, gave the team direction. The leadership's integrity is challenged the most when adversity is the greatest. Research supports this. In study after study, employees consistently explain that their leaders are willing to put them in unsafe situations to get a job or task done. Saying one thing in good times and abandoning those principles in tough times degrades your integrity. Integrity doesn't work that way. You either have it or you don't. Without it, effective leadership is impossible.

Integrity keeps everyone on the same page when it comes to behavioral expectations. As the leader you must say to your team, "We will keep our word."

Integrity is the foundation that every other leadership trait sits on.

The word *integral*, from which the word *integrity* is derived, reinforces the idea. The definition of *integral* is "necessary to make a whole complete; essential or fundamental."[3] Fairness, honesty, keeping your word, and trustworthiness are necessary to maintain your integrity.

The concepts in this book will not help you if you don't commit to leading with integrity in everything you do and in every situation you face. Doing this is up to one person: you.

---

[3] "Integral," Google's English dictionary, Oxford Languages.

CHAPTER SIX

TRUST

My wife has a large, pure jade carving of a dragon given to her by her mother who acquired it years ago when she visited China. When our youngest son, Brayden, was five, he was playing hide-and-seek with his older brother, Pierce. He hid in the living room under the coffee table, where the jade dragon sat. In his excitement to run, Brayden jumped up and the dragon took flight, crashing to the ground and breaking into three pieces. After tears were shed and apologies made and accepted, my wife glued the dragon back together and put it in a closet. You have to look closely to see the damage; however, she never took the dragon out of hiding. It went from being a beautifully displayed piece of art to being defective. While the sentimental value is still there, it just isn't the same.

When I was eighteen years old, my stepfather allowed me to use his car to go to prom. It was a brand-new 1974 Lincoln Continental. He'd had it for four months. That car was gorgeous—I was surprised he trusted me to drive it. Everything was going great. I got my date to the prom safely. On the way home, I was going through an intersection when a man ran a red light and hit the car, destroying the front end. There were no injuries, but the other driver and I were in total shock about the car. I was so worried about disappointing my stepfather. He was a very gracious and trusting man.

When I got home, my stepfather came out and looked at the car and said, "Well, that's why there are repair shops." He didn't hold the accident against me (and if he did, I couldn't tell). The car was repaired and you couldn't tell it had been hit, but it was never the same. Each time I walked past the car, in my mind, I could still see the damage.

When trust is broken it often can be repaired. However, trust is like the jade dragon and the Continental. Once it's damaged, things are never the same between individuals. You both know it's been broken.

I've talked about integrity, ethics, listening, and fairness. These are some of the ingredients you'll need in your "recipe" for building trust. If any of these ingredients are missing, you will not be able to build trusting relationships with your team.

Trust is the outcome of your work using the skills I talk about in this book. You can't learn trust—you can only maintain the values and develop the skills needed in building trust. Developing trust is the sum of all of your daily interactions. However, you can destroy trust through a single interaction. A lack of integrity, ethics, or honesty can break trust in a moment.

GAINING THE TRUST OF THE DISGRUNTLED, BITTER, OR ANTI-ESTABLISHMENT EMPLOYEE

I've attended numerous workshops that were focused on teaching leaders how to build workplace trust. These workshops are typically designed with the express intent of highlighting the values that are needed to establish trust. They also point out how negative and impactful a lack of trust in the workforce can be on the company's bottom line. But I never found or attended a workshop that taught leaders how to move a disgruntled employee toward trust. How do you get a team of employees who are anti-company to trust you?

Today, there are trust issues between groups that are highlighted in the media on a daily basis. Some Starbucks and Amazon employees want to unionize. Political parties are warring, and neighbors can't even bear the sight of one another if they have opposing political signs in their yards. These are all cases of distrust. Distrust also exists within individual workgroups and companies. You are most certainly going to experience situations where there is distrust by association. The employees will see you as an extension of the organization. That being said, even in these circumstances you can build trust with your team. You cannot erase the damage, but you can put the pieces back together. You can build a path based on your values and your terms and conditions.

Your objectives as a supervisor are to have your team achieve the organization's goals daily. When there is trust between the supervisor and their teams, there are better outcomes. According to a 2017

Harvard Business Review article, high-trust companies reported 74 percent less stress, 106 percent more energy at work, 50 percent higher productivity, 13 percent fewer sick days, 76 percent more engagement, 29 percent more life satisfaction, and 40 percent less burnout.[1]

In other words: Trust matters. And it's not always easy to come by. It takes time. For example, I have owned a 1965 Mustang for twenty-four years and have fully restored it. Finding mechanics to work on it has always been a challenge. The mechanic I have today works on all of our vehicles and he is someone I completely trust with my car repairs, even the Mustang's. Did that happen the first time I took a car to him? No. Our relationship was purely transactional in the beginning. I needed some work done and he provided a service. Over time, my experiences with him built trust. He has always kept his word, did what he promised he would do at the cost he committed to, communicated effectively when things changed, and has been honest with me. He satisfied my terms and conditions to do business with someone. Therefore, he is trustworthy. On occasion when I could not pick the

---

[1] Paul J. Zak, "The Neuroscience of Trust," *Harvard Business Review*, January-February 2017, 84–90, https://hbr.org/2017/01/the-neuroscience-of-trust.

car up, he drove it to my home. He parked it in the garage, locked the garage, and left the keys inside of the car. He had my best interest in mind. He made the effort to build trust with me.

Not every repair on the Mustang went as expected. On one occasion I had to have the car towed, and the same problem resurfaced after it had already been repaired. It was a tremendous inconvenience. But I didn't assign the car's failure to my mechanic's lack of concern or caring. I knew he cared and that he believed the work he'd done would fix the problem. I believed this because I trusted him.

Trust is developed over time. This makes it different from other values-based areas. The first time we meet I can listen to what you say. I can be honest, fair, and ethical. After the first meeting, if you were asked if I listened to you, you could say yes or no. However, if you were asked if you trust me, the answer would be, "I don't know him well enough yet," because you do not. Even if you do everything you can to display terms and conditions that are forthright in the initial meeting, at that point, you cannot establish trust completely.

I had a manager early in my career who developed distrust in his initial meeting with my peers and me. He was extremely self-centered and had a somewhat narcissistic personality. He let us know that there was a new sheriff in town and that our previous results were unacceptable and would no longer be tolerated. This all came out within the first three minutes of the meeting. He accomplished his goal. He created fear within the group. As a result, we developed behaviors to defend ourselves, and we *never* trusted a single word he had to say. We did our jobs, always keeping his threats in mind, while documenting our interactions with him. When it was possible, we avoided meeting alone with him. The morale of the team fell drastically.

Bad morale never produces great results.

Thankfully he was replaced as our leader within a year. (Note: It's typically easier to replace the coach than the entire team.) In three minutes, he had guaranteed that he would not get support. He let the jade dragon and the Lincoln Continental stay broken, and he never even tried to repair them.

Distrust can be established during a first

meeting, as can the foundation for building trust. Building trust starts immediately by establishing the terms and conditions of values-based leadership principles. You must communicate the importance of these values up front, then live by them.

The best way to get people to follow you as a leader is to walk the walk, not just talk the talk.

REPAIRING TRUST AFTER YOU HAVE BROKEN IT

All leaders make mistakes with their teams. I made more than my share of mistakes. On my second day at one job, I was assigned to retrain a poor-performing employee. I was not skilled in any aspect of leadership. My approach was to let the employee know that I was there to enforce the company's standards. I did not use a positive approach toward the employee; instead, I criticized him and his work performance. He immediately developed distrust toward me. In his mind, I was also attacking his character (aka his humanity). He defended himself, and instead of getting better at his job, he got worse.

The employee's reaction wasn't surprising. It was a perfectly rational response. It made sense. We were both distrustful and negative as I had set the tone.

Fortunately, before the situation got too out of hand, my manager challenged the approach I was using. He taught me a better approach that would improve the outcome, not hamper it.

I sat down with the employee after a few days, and we came to an agreement that was workable. I did my best to repair the damage I had caused. Just as my son apologized to my wife for the broken jade statue, I apologized and admitted my initial error and my part in breaking the employee's trust.

Over an extended period, our relationship improved, but it didn't happen overnight. Just as my mechanic proved to me, through his efforts and good faith, that I could trust him with my Mustang, I proved to the employee that I had his best interests in mind and wanted to see him do well. As time went on, we even had a laugh together. However, it was never going to be what it could have been had I not made such a lousy first impression. The damage to the relationship was in many ways like the Lincoln Continental or the jade dragon. The employee had forgiven me. However, we both knew what happened and it was a reminder for me to be more careful in the future. My apology and sincere effort to change over time helped heal our relationship.

In 1959, Jim Casey said, "Once the people you deal with come to recognize that what you do springs from an honest heart, they will be surprisingly strong in their support of you.

"They will give you their loyalty.

"They will trust and follow you.

"In short you will win their confidence, even to the extent that they will forgive whatever mistakes you make."

As a leader you will make mistakes. You may even cause some damage. It is important to make an honest, forthright attempt to repair some of that damage. Your people will see your honesty of purpose and you will win their support.

EXERCISES

A. On a notepad list three people you trust completely and why you trust them. What qualities do they possess? What makes these qualities important to you?

B. Make a list of the top three terms and conditions needed to establish trust with you.

C. List two people you distrust and the reasons you distrust each of them. What are commonalities between the two?

CHAPTER SEVEN

PROVIDING CONSISTENT FEEDBACK

ONE OF THE MOST rewarding activities I have engaged in is mentoring young leaders. One of my mentees, JoAnn, is a thirty-year-old project engineer. She is enthusiastic, committed to her work (perhaps to a fault), and brilliant. We meet monthly and typically speak about whatever topic she chooses. In one instance, she wanted to discuss the review of a presentation she had given to senior management. It was on the development and deployment of a new piece of technology in Europe.

While she was building the presentation, she spoke frequently about it. I have sat through hundreds of presentations as a senior leader. She would rehearse it with me as her audience and I would provide feedback. I knew she had applied a tremendous amount of effort to ensure its success. The presentation took her quite some time to put together. She agonized over it every step of the way.

JoAnn was very disappointed in the feedback she received during and after the presentation. There was no verbal feedback given at the meeting indicating whether they were pleased or displeased. She took their silence negatively. In her view senior management must have been unhappy. She believed the adage "If you have nothing good to say, then say nothing" was applicable to their lack of response.

About a week later, JoAnn's boss let her know that she had done a great job. The attendees were impressed with her and the content of the presentation. This was fortunate. Had he continued to be silent, the experience would have had a lasting impact on JoAnn. Her attitude understandably reversed, demonstrating that providing feedback to your team can be a powerful tool.

FEEDBACK IS MORE THAN THE WORDS YOU SPEAK

Every action you take with your team is feedback. Even no feedback is feedback. As the leader, your role is to develop your team's abilities to accomplish the organization's objectives. Areas like great customer service, performance, using proper methods, engagement, and support for the organization's goals—all stem from how you, the leader, coach, develop, and provide feedback to your people. As you work with your team, give feedback daily, not occasionally. This is what good leaders do.

I've consistently seen new leaders start the job as order givers and task assigners. When you perform your duties in this manner, you are not being a leader. You are being a human memo. We literally have AI apps for that on our phones. Do you want to be replaced by an app?

The leader's role extends well beyond giving out assignments and managing tasks. You are also charged with motivating, encouraging, and responding to the needs of the team. When employees do a good job, a leader must give feedback and recognize the employee for it. Likewise, when a leader is training an employee, they need to give feedback in order to help them develop their skills. Throughout my career, I've worked with hundreds of newly promoted supervisors. I've seen few who knew how to provide critical and necessary feedback in the absence of training and practice in this skill.

When onboarding employees, safety training is one of the most basic requirements. Annual certifications for existing employees are also an important requirement.

On one occasion I attended a safety review being held by Ken, our local safety manager. He was responsible for working with the business units that were experiencing high injury rates. He'd chosen one that was led by a manager named Don. The employees assigned to this particular operation were incurring injuries at twice the rate of their peer groups.

As the meeting began, Don opened with some comments emphasizing all the activities that his team had put into place to address the safety issues. He explained that each of the supervisors under him would be covering a specific action item. Don had managed this unit of just over one hundred employees for two years, so he was very familiar with them.

Ken asked Don if we could see the employee records before any presentations were given. He became observably nervous at this request. I expected this reaction. Ken explained to Don and his team, "I think it's important for me as the safety manager to know how we can support your efforts better. The employee safety training records always tell us where we need to go, so I would like Noel and I to see them."

After some examination, I saw that some of the employees had excellent safety training engagements and others did not. I noticed that the records for the employees assigned to Jan, one of Don's supervisors, were detailed. They were comprehensive and included great feedback and coaching comments. Jan had detailed where the employees were deficient in a particular skill and had coached them on improving that skill. As a result, her employees were not being injured at the rate of the other supervisors' groups. Jan didn't just give her employees the poison—she provided them with the antidote. As a result, they weren't getting injured. Ken and I looked at the records together, and we both complimented Jan on the excellent training she had provided.

Jan's peers were not providing coaching feedback to their employees on *how* to get better, so they weren't getting better. Her peers would work with employees only after they had sustained an injury. This is a reactive approach. Jan's approach was proactive. In Stephen Covey's book *The 7 Habits of Highly Effective People*, a book I recommend all leaders read, the first habit is to be proactive, and Jan was.

Providing daily feedback is one of the most challenging aspects of leadership. In the infancy of a leadership career, the desire to avoid conflict is common. Supervisors want their people to like them. Discussions about improving performance can be intimidating and are often avoided. The position, however, requires letting employees know when they are doing something below the required standard. It also requires letting them know when they are doing things right or exceptionally. I generally saw supervisors giving positive or negative feedback off the cuff. They would see an employee do something wrong or have someone who was ineffective at the job, and out of frustration they would make a reactive comment without considering its impact. Nothing regarding employee feedback should be done or said off the cuff. All words matter! Reactive feedback can create unintended negative consequences. Negative attitudes follow negative comments, it's that simple.

Another behavior I saw regularly was supervisors using terms of endearment with their employees, such as "Hey, man," "Hey, buddy," "Hey, pal," and "Hey there," or phrases such as "Can you do me a favor?" These phrases aren't professional, and they don't help you to develop a professional relationship. This language sends a message to some individuals that you have a personal relationship with them. You can develop positive, upbeat relationships with your teams, but you are not their friend. Behavior like this can create blurred lines. When someone requires discipline, you are the one who will pay the price for any misunderstanding. The best relationships between a supervisor and their team contain mutual respect and courtesy, and they are always professional. These are the terms and conditions that work when leading. Keeping the lines straight and maintaining your professionalism protects everyone.

Remember: Familiarity breeds contempt. Extensive knowledge of or close association with someone or something leads to a loss of respect for them or it.

This phrase is pointing out a natural occurrence with regard to relationships: They are more respectful in the beginning than over the long term. Think about when you first met your spouse, partner, or boss. After a while, a comfort sets in. Things that would not be said in the beginning are now said easily. You are prone to take the other person for granted, and judgments follow.

For the better part of thirty years, I used the phrase "familiarity breeds contempt" often with those I led as managers and supervisors. The impetus would be that there was an incident or event that had occurred between them and one of their people. A relationship had emerged that lacked professionalism. The employee believed the manager or supervisor turned a blind eye, let things slide. In these cases, I had the supervisor or manager look up the definition of *contempt* and read it aloud. They always cringed while reading it; *contempt* is a tough word. We would discuss this further after they'd read it.

After our discussion there would be an aha moment when they realized that the respect they needed as the leader had been compromised. Familiarity should not breed a lack of professionalism.

For the leader to provide feedback that is respected, they must be respected professionally by their team members.

The leader's role is to develop their team as a coach. When you watch coaches, they stand on the sideline, encouraging and congratulating players who are playing well *during* the game. They coach "live" and provide constant feedback on the spot. They don't take time off in the middle of the game. They don't even leave for a restroom break! Coaching while being with their teams in the moment is *that* important. Effective leaders stay on the field with their teams during the game.

EVERYONE NEEDS A COACH

Tom Brady, who's won seven Super Bowls, still has a coach. Michael Jordan, who many believe is the greatest athlete to have played any sport, had a coach. No matter how great a player is, they still need a coach. Everyone needs outside perspectives to improve. Your role is to provide feedback, like the coach during the game. Leaders must master two types of feedback: *motivational* and *formative*.

Motivational Feedback: This type of feedback recognizes the employees' strengths and accomplishments. The purpose is to acknowledge the employees' efforts, to thank them for playing well. If you are working with them on their skills, this feedback is essential during those sessions.

Formative Feedback: This is developmental feedback, which focuses on opportunities to improve. Feedback should be positive and reinforcing. It should help your team learn to play better.

The way you deliver feedback will determine how well your employees accept and use your coaching. Do it well and they get better. Do it poorly and they get worse and perhaps even become resentful.

The Four to One (4:1) Feedback Ratio is considered the most successful way to provide feedback. Simply put, this concept states: People need to receive at least four positive inputs on their behavior for every one corrective input. This ensures they will respond and put forth their best effort.

In his book *Bringing Out the Best in People*, author Aubrey Daniels breaks down the 4:1 ratio and shares the science and data behind it. Reinforcing what an employee does well acknowledges their efforts, which opens them up to receiving and adopting developmental input. I was introduced to the concept in the mid-1990s and have used it ever since.

When applied to our own life experiences, it is not difficult to understand why this technique is effective. Criticism stings. No one likes hearing they are doing things wrong or substandard, and this can be particularly annoying if they are called out daily. When the poison is delivered with no antidote, there is no motivation to improve. Even the most unproductive employee is doing something positive that deserves acknowledgment. Your role in coaching and providing feedback to your people is knowing what they do well. It is not your role to focus only on their errors and mistakes.

So how do you let employees know how they are doing in areas beyond those kept on a spreadsheet? It starts with keeping organized notes on your employees after you work with them. I found it impossible to recall the positive accomplishments that happened over a three-, six-, or twelve-month period for a group of employees. In fact, I never had an employee say to me, "You only acknowledge my positive actions, never my negative ones!"

The truth is, we are all experts in tracking defects. Most companies do that well, even small ones. Employees do the work and produce daily results, and therefore anything that needs to get better is the focus of those daily results. Supervisors often focus on what did not go right or well. I did not attend many meetings where the complete attention was on how we were recognizing individual employees' accomplishments.

I learned from a mentor early in my career to include in my daily planner notes throughout the year employees' positive accomplishments. Today's technology provides multiple programs, such as apps, that simplify capturing and retaining this information. In our lives we do the things we care about. The same holds true in leadership. Good leaders care enough about their people's positive daily accomplishments to keep track of them.

Applying the 4:1 ratio while providing formative and motivational feedback takes practice. It is a difficult skill to master. But practice makes perfect, as the saying goes. Begin using the skill by mastering 2:1, then 3:1, and so on. Using the method will help you build up your people.

EXERCISES

A. Practice using the 4:1 ratio with friends and family. Let them know what you're doing and why.

Observe how family members perform small household chores and tasks such as taking out the trash, changing a light bulb, or opening a can of vegetables—anything will do to practice using the 4:1 ratio. As this individual performs the task, write down the positives you observe and one area where improvement may be necessary. Use motivational and formative feedback in a 4:1 fashion.

B. Complete an abbreviated performance review on a newer employee.

Let the employee know at least one day prior that you will be conducting a short review. Set a positive atmosphere with the employee during the notification. State a few positives, such as, "John, you're doing a nice job in many areas, and tomorrow, I'd like to review your progress." When a supervisor uses motivational feedback to arrange the review, the employee's defenses are lowered. This allows the door for formative feedback to open.

C. List all the positives that you have, including hard data and your observations. Ask the employee to share their view of their current performance. Highlight the positives they mention and the areas where they believe they can improve.

D. Review at least four of their positives and provide correlating motivational feedback. Review only one area needing development, using formative feedback.

E. Offer your assistance to help the employee improve. Ask them what they would like from you. Write down what they say, show it to them, and then agree on the next steps.

In summary, keep these words of Jim Casey in mind: "One measure of your success will be the degree to which you build up others who work with you. While building up others, you will build up yourself."

CHAPTER EIGHT

OWNERSHIP AND TAKING RESPONSIBILITY

When my sons were teenagers living at home, keeping them balanced between online gaming and schoolwork was a constant battle. One (not recommended) method I used on my younger son was leveraging his desires for gaming to get him to do other, more responsible things. In other words, we engaged in a bit of tit for tat. If he did what I asked, I rewarded him. In one instance, there was a hot new gaming system he wanted badly. After we reached a mutual agreement, we purchased it for his birthday. Within less than a year, the system was no longer good enough, and it sat in a box unused. He hadn't contributed to the purchase price, so he had no ownership of it. It collected dust until we donated the system to a nonprofit organization.

Today my son holds a master's degree from the Berklee College of Music and is an audio engineer. He has a studio in his home that he built from scratch. It has a high-quality sound booth and sound editing equipment worth well over fifty thousand dollars. He paid for it all with his hard work and prudent saving habits. No one is allowed to touch, let alone use, his equipment. After he'd finished designing and building his studio, he wanted me to see it. I can attest it is first class, as fine as any used to edit first-rate productions. It is evident that he has clear ownership for what he worked for and created. None of his equipment will end up in an unopened box or ever go unused! That's what ownership does. It creates a connection between the creator and the created.

While I was the president for UPS in Chicago, I had an operation in Harvey, Illinois, with twenty-five employees who were facing a major change in their supply chain design. Our engineering team was responsible for presenting the design change to Ed, the manager of the Harvey team. Both Ed and the engineering team would then present the change to the workgroup. As their leader, I attended both meetings.

As soon as the engineers and managers finished presenting, they faced resistance. The employees clearly did not support the change. During the meeting, one very influential employee stated loudly, "This change won't work! It will slow us down!" Other employees joined in, and before long there was a chorus of complaints.

Essentially, the change required them to add a new destination to their distribution pattern. The objection was *how* it was being done. The engineers weren't expecting this reaction, and the meeting began to deteriorate quickly. In order to control the meeting, Ed interjected. He said firmly to his team that they would be making the change as requested, because, as he put it, "We do what is expected of us." Ed took pride and ownership in everything he was responsible for and he expected his people to do the same. UPS needed the change, and he expected them to make it work.

At that point I whispered to Ed, "Why don't you get their suggestions on how the required change *should* be done? Then let's review what comes from that."

The next day we met. Ed reviewed what his employees wanted, which was no change to the operation's current design. The engineering group and Ed objected to leaving the design as it was. I let Ed and the engineers know that as much as I appreciated their position, we would go with the employees' wishes. Ed stated, "Noel, I don't agree with that. They need to know sometimes we will make changes, and it's not up to them."

I responded, "Ed, that's true. However, realize this: **People naturally support the things they create. They won't let their plan fail. They will let *your* plan fail, but never theirs.** Add the additional position where they want it and leave it at that. What is important here, Ed, is that they see *you* as the one letting them have their own plan, which they won't see as being influenced by anyone else. Your support is what matters, not mine." We both suspected their plan would fail, but if we were going to get them to have buy-in to the engineer's plan, they needed to get to the point where they saw their own plan come up short.

Ed agreed, and the change was made as scheduled. Unsurprisingly, the employees found out quickly that their plan was not working. They had to work much harder than needed to execute it. Their pride, however, wouldn't allow them to admit it. So they stuck with it for three days. It was comical on a few levels. Although they made all of the schedules for the new position on time, it required an extraordinary effort. The engineers had given them a plan where the transition would be smooth, but they had rejected that plan. On the fourth day, the employees let Ed know that they would like to try the engineers' plan after all. Ed called me and let me know about the employees' request. Ed and I both laughed. I said, "I'm surprised it took this long for them to request the return to the engineer's plan." The change engineering suggested was implemented. The employees took ownership for it from that point forward, and it went like clockwork.

It is human nature for people who have a routine that they like or prefer to reject any attempt to change it. Employees I have led have only positively accepted a change when it benefited them personally. Changes made by the company are generally met with resistance. As their leader, you should always anticipate and plan the approach you will use when presenting change to your team. In this case, an outcome was needed, and achieving that outcome was all that really mattered. *That is all that ever matters.* The execution of the change has to be open for discussion with the people who will be doing the work. When the employees were allowed to use their plan, they took ownership and had a stake in succeeding. Their commitment benefited both the manager and the company. For plans to work well, they need employee buy-in. You can give instructions, directions, and even orders to individuals or a team. However, w*hat you can't do is force their emotional support.* Emotional support develops from collaboration and inclusion, and when the employee has a stake in the outcome.

In 2003, while I was the president of UPS in Virginia, the area experienced the Category 4 hurricane Isabel. There was extreme flooding and treefall. In its aftermath roads became impassable for well over a month. However, after the hurricane had passed, our team went into emergency conditions planning. The engineers assessed the conditions around the state and developed a series of plans that would be used. All managers received the plans, and conference calls were held to communicate the plan and help move it forward. These plans were then expected to be reviewed with all employees.

I went to a meeting where well over a hundred delivery drivers were in attendance to review the plans. It was led by Frank, the manager of the group, and Ken, the safety manager. They had prepared handouts for everyone present. As the handouts were circulated throughout the room, I could see disagreement on the employees' faces. Many would look at the handouts and begin rolling their eyes, whispering to the person next to them or shaking their heads. They were showing all the signs. The lights were flashing: *hazard ahead!*

An employee with over thirty-five years of seniority stood and spoke up respectfully.

"Frank, you guys don't seem to understand that half of the stuff on this sheet won't work. Most of the roads are impassable, including where we live. Our own homes have been damaged, we don't have running water, and the schools are closed so our children are at home. We have entire sections of the city we can't even access, yet in this plan you are asking us to go into areas that we know aren't fully accessible. You're also asking us to be here by 7:30 a.m. to get a jump on things, I suppose. However, some people can't get out of their own areas until they are let out. We don't control that."

Frank stopped reviewing the plans when he saw that his team was upset. He knew when people get upset, they don't listen. Frank apologized to his team openly: "Listen, everyone, I have always valued your input. That didn't change today, and it has not changed—things had to move swiftly. In the haste of making plans, Ken and I disregarded the importance of getting your feedback."

He added: "We must get the job done. You all know that there are hospitals, nursing homes, elderly people waiting for medications, and they are depending on us to get their supplies to them, especially now. We will do it safely, and in the best manner possible without putting any of you in a tough situation."

Frank took ownership of the error in front of his team first and he didn't pass the buck. Nor did he give up and completely capitulate to the upset team.

He set the tone. The employees knew they would be included going forward on any potential solutions, so they immediately quieted down. Frank then asked the employees for five volunteers to assist him in developing a plan. Not surprisingly, over thirty hands went up.

Frank and the volunteers developed guidelines to review with their team. All of the company's guidelines were adhered to. Some were modified, but none was disregarded. This was presented to the group with Frank leading the meeting. There was clear support from the team as a result.

Frank accomplished the things that needed to be accomplished because he was skilled and an experienced manager. He saw the signs and reacted to them. He knew that if his people did not support the direction, there would be resentment, leading to negative outcomes. No leader should allow a negative environment to stay negative. Leaders have a direct responsibility to prevent that.

Later that day on a conference call with all business units, I had Frank recount what had happened. Other managers heard Frank's story and noted they had experienced the same discourse from their teams.

The process of getting employee feedback on all emergency plans was implemented throughout all business units moving forward.

At UPS we were good at getting feedback on the day-to-day aspects of the business. However, when emergencies arose, this wasn't a uniform practice. After this, we decided to lay out a plan and apply it across the board. In later reviews, other managers spoke about how they had followed Frank's approach. They involved their people in developing the plans so things went safely and smoothly.

This is not to say employees get to decide what direction is taken or what outcome is needed. No leader should abdicate their responsibility. The company expects the leader to own the outcomes produced by their teams. The leader (you) will fare far better getting support when employees believe you respect their abilities to contribute. They will take ownership when you open the door to participation.

When employees feel included, they feel important. People support what they help to create.

EXERCISES

On a notepad answer these questions:

A. As an employee, have you ever been in a situation where changes that affected your role were made, but you weren't consulted? How did that make you feel?

B. Think of a time when a leader you worked under solicited input from the team about changes to processes and procedures. What was the team's response?

C. As a leader, has there ever been a time when you didn't ask for your team's input on something? What was their response? How could you have handled the situation differently?

PART TWO

THE FINE PRINT: PUTTING VALUE-BASED LEADERSHIP INTO PRACTICE

CHAPTER NINE

BUILDING EMPLOYEES' SKILLS AND KEEPING YOUR TEAM

ONE OF THE BIGGEST outcomes of the pandemic is among the corporate world, and it is being dubbed "The Great Resignation," "The Big Quit," or "The Great Reshuffle." If you drove down any street in a business district in America in 2022, you'd see an abundance of Help Wanted signs. The unemployment rate in the US in 2022 was 3.6 percent, one of the lowest in US history at the time. During the pandemic and due to quarantine lockdowns, working from home became the norm. For many Americans, this created a desire to continue working from home after the pandemic restrictions lifted. Companies struggled to recruit employees because of the fierce competition for them. They also had a difficult time retaining employees, who had many choices for employment.

As the leader, in order to keep employees, you must meet their "demands"—in other words, their terms and conditions.

From the time I started my career in 1977 until I retired in 2019, employee retention at UPS was consistently a top-five priority. Retention was so critical it was a metric on all operations management performance reviews, including my own as a president. This has not changed. Retention can never be ignored, in good times or bad.

The preciousness of keeping employees was amplified during the years immediately following the pandemic, but it was not a new concept. Constant employee turnover guarantees inconsistent results for the company and the customer. This is why CEOs in the vast majority of companies, not just UPS, rank talent management—which includes retention—as a top priority. Companies invest billions of dollars annually in the hiring and initial training of employees. It can be extremely costly for a company if a fully trained employee leaves shortly after being hired. That's why leaders who know how to retain their employees and keep them satisfied and motivated are highly valued: Retention affects the company's bottom line. **These leaders understand that people don't quit companies, they quit people. The people they quit are typically their supervisors or managers.**

When I started working for UPS, I was hired to work in a distribution hub at night loading trailers. The job was part-time, and it was meant to be three to four hours a night. I was nineteen and a college student, so I thought it would be perfect for my schedule. I could work from 11:00 p.m. until 3:00 a.m., get a few hours of sleep, and get to my first class, which started at 10:00 a.m. My class load for my major, electrical engineering, was fairly heavy and challenging.

On my first night, the supervisor paired me with another employee named Kevin who would show me the job. We would be lifting and loading packages weighing up to fifty pounds each. He wanted me to know that the first week would result in lots of sore muscles. I was in good physical shape and had no concerns. Kevin was right. The job was a physical workout for three to five hours straight. I was sweating through all of my clothes, head to toe. As it neared 3:00 a.m., I was looking forward to ending my first day, but my supervisor didn't release me. Instead, we were let go at 7:00 a.m. Since class started at ten, I drove straight to school. Exhausted, I fell asleep in my physics class. Afterward, I went home and slept until it was time to leave for work.

My second and third nights were a repeat of the first night. On the fourth night in the middle of the shift, I'd had it. I stopped loading packages and decided to walk out.

"Kevin, good luck, but I am leaving and going home," I said.

"Noel, you can't quit! You said you needed this job to pay your tuition. It will get better. I guarantee it! Give it some time," Kevin exclaimed.

"No, Kevin, I'm quitting."

Kevin summoned the supervisor, Nick (who wasn't much older than I was), to come over. I explained my position to Nick and said I was done.

"Each night I am putting all of my efforts into making things work out. I am not willing to sacrifice my studies for this job," I explained.

Nick asked me if I could wait a few minutes.

"Sure," I said.

He sent me to the employee break room, and I waited for him there.

Nick entered and went to the vending machine and bought me a Coke. He said if he had known I had such an early class, he would have made it a priority to get me out by 4:00 a.m. He felt I was doing great for only having been on the job three days. He knew it was tough, but he felt I had what it took to become an excellent employee.

"Do me a favor, Noel. Give it at least another week. You are doing better than any employee I have had in their first three days. The other employees really like you as well. Kevin thinks you are great too. I am confident things will smooth out in our work area and I will get you out by 3:00 to 4:00 a.m.," Nick said.

I agreed to give it another week, and I appreciated Nick taking the time to speak with me.

Nick kept his word and got me out on my school days by 4:00 a.m. And I kept my word, staying another week. I never looked back after that. If it hadn't been for Nick, I would not have had any career at UPS. Until he stepped in, the terms and conditions UPS set with me had been violated.

I would venture to say that my experience is not that unique. Most people will want to quit or stop coming when their terms and conditions are not met. It wasn't the business unit president, the division manager, or the manager who kept me there—Nick did. **The supervisor matters more than all three of those individuals combined when it comes to keeping a new employee.**

PEOPLE DON'T QUIT COMPANIES, THEY QUIT PEOPLE

Nick, acting of his own volition, prevented me, a UPS employee, from quitting. This was when there were no metrics driving his actions. He simply cared enough to take an approach to make a connection. This was quite unusual for a twenty-year-old running a loading dock. I was fortunate that he was the first person I worked for.

When an employee is hired, they have terms and conditions, and when those are violated, they will "fire" their immediate boss by quitting.

The top employee expectations in business today are:

- Positive work culture
- Recognition
- Work–life balance
- Respect and trust
- Transparency and honesty
- Constructive feedback

No matter what list you look at or survey you read (and I have read dozens), they all state the same thing: Employees have *specific* terms and conditions to be met. When they are hired, they know the pay rate and the hours of work that will be required. That is why these two items are not at the top of any list you will see. All employees you lead expect their emotional terms and conditions to be met by you. Not the company or your boss—*you*. **If your employees are turning over at a high rate, you must take ownership and correct it.** This starts with training your employees properly as well as getting to know them personally. It starts with *caring enough*—the way Nick cared about me.

TRAINING AND DEVELOPMENT

When I was ten years old my brother and I went to our local Boys Club of America twice a week. We took boxing lessons there and were members of the pre-sixteen boxing team. Our coach, Bill Glass, a volunteer, was an amazing man. He would go on to become a coach for the US Olympic Boxing team. Bill made certain that the members of his team understood that you can accomplish whatever you have put the *work in* to accomplish. If you don't put the work in, don't expect to win in boxing or anything you do. What I came to appreciate about Bill later in my life is that he was teaching me how to be successful. Jim Casey said it a different way: "You can't hope to get more than you give." Jim was explaining that if you don't invest in developing your people, building their skills or their confidence, why would you expect a solid return from them?

You shouldn't expect a solid return from employees you haven't invested in, but many leaders do.

Boxing matches are based on one criterion—your weight class. It was common for a twelve-year-old, for instance, to be in a match with a thirteen-year-old boy if they weighed the same. Boys Clubs would compete against other Boys Clubs, and it was not always possible to match kids' weights exactly for a boxing match. There was one instance when Bill let me know that I would be boxing against a fourteen-year-old who outweighed me by ten pounds. He pointed to the kid I would be boxing and then I looked at Bill.

"I can't beat that kid!" I said.

"Who do I have you practice against?" Bill asked.

"Anthony, Coach."

"How old is Anthony?"

"Fourteen, but he's not as big as that kid!"

"You've practiced against Anthony, and I know you are prepared for this."

Bill then put his hand on my shoulder.

"If you don't want to do it, then I won't force you. I don't know that you'll win, but I am confident it will make you better and that you'll do well," he said.

I agreed to box the fourteen-year-old. Bill showed confidence in me, and that's what good leaders do. It was more confidence than I had in myself. He also had prepared me. He had coached me for four years.

Whenever we trained, Bill demonstrated the maneuvers one at a time. He had us work on *one thing* until we got it right. This is how he taught us to defend ourselves from any number of angles and punches. One angle, one punch at a time. He demonstrated each move, and then we each had to mimic his move. We would repeat that pattern over and over and over, until we got an angle or a punch down. You could not *almost* get it right with Coach Bill; you had to demonstrate getting that one thing right before going to the next thing. When you did get it right, he'd celebrate it with comments to build your confidence, such as, "You got it! I knew you could do it!" He was confident in having me box an older and larger boxer because he knew what he had put into me, so he knew what he would get out of me.

It is important to note that Bill did not put any boxer at risk. We wore safety gear that made us look like the Pillsbury Doughboy—full headgear, oversized gloves, and a body jacket. There was no bodily risk to me with a larger fighter.

I won the bout unanimously, and it was a

turning point in my life. You can't know you are going to win every match in boxing. What I did know is that Bill always had me prepared. After the bout with the fourteen-year-old, I had confidence that if I put in the work and listened to my coach, I would be tough to beat. I went on that year to win the overall Boys Club title for my weight class. I won in the finals against a boxer who had defeated my older brother the previous year. He was a year older, four inches taller, and five pounds heavier than I was. Without a coach like Bill Glass, that win likely wouldn't have happened. My discipline and values around preparation as an adult came from the man who was my coach as a child. Bill Glass had a lot to do with why I rose to a senior management level in a Fortune 500 company.

PRIMACY: WHAT YOU LEARN FIRST, YOU REMEMBER THE BEST AND RETAIN THE LONGEST

Primacy is a critical concept to remember when developing employees. This starts with their initial training. Most supervisors see training a new employee to do the job as just another task. A task is a physical activity. Training an employee is an emotional activity—it is not a task! During the training of a new employee, you have an opportunity to communicate the terms and conditions you and the employee have with each other. This includes a values-based conversation along with their job training. Here you have the opportunity to develop their primacy and create a lasting, core memory that they will carry with them always. You'll do this by building their confidence, helping them to become a valued team member, and demonstrating to them what success looks like. You are their coach.

Companies generally have a protocol for bringing on new employees, though some do not. Usually, the job basics are covered. These are intended to orient the employee and get them to produce work as quickly as possible. Getting them up to speed quickly matters. However, this can't be at the expense of quality training. Remember, the rule of primacy dictates that whatever you teach them in the beginning will become the basis for how they will perform the job forever. *Teach them wrong and they stay wrong; teach them right and they stay right.*

The most effective process I have experienced for training employees is the **7 Steps for Effective Direct Training**. This includes the following:

1. Demonstrate each separate step of the job.

2. Have the employee describe each step you performed back to you.

3. Ask and answer questions.

4. Have the employee perform the job while you guide them.

5. Provide feedback.

6. Have the employee demonstrate what was taught while they describe what they are doing. Repeat until they are 100 percent successful.

7. Monitor the employee while they're on the job to ensure learning is effective.

This is exactly what Bill Glass did as a coach, even though he didn't realize it. He was using the seven steps of effective training. He demonstrated each maneuver and then had us demonstrate it. He had each boxer do it again and again while explaining what it would accomplish or why. He asked us to explain it to him after we had done it. I have vivid memories of many of those moments. I can close my eyes and see Bill standing there demonstrating a technique that I was shown fifty years ago. That is how powerful training should be. When you train an employee, your objective should be the same as Bill's was.

When the seven steps of effective training are used in their totality, employees know the job. As their coach and leader, you must have them perform the skills in a continuous loop until they master them. This technique works, and primacy ensures they will retain it.

KNOW WHAT YOU DON'T KNOW, THEN GET TO KNOW IT

More than ever, employers rely on technology to train employees. There are some great simulations available. In the area of safety training, employees can experience situations that create accidents and learn how to avoid them. I've supported having technology developed to train employees for these reasons. Most certifications today are done with some form of video training.

This makes sense and has improved the efficiency of those processes. The use of AI will only amplify this. Technology, however, will not completely replace direct training with an employee. That's your job, and that will never go away. When an employee watches a video for training, always be sure to use the seven steps of training to assess whether that training was effective. If you do not, then you don't know that they actually know, and it is your role to know.

The organization will hire and give you employees. You must own your role in integrating the employee's emotional needs and strengths into the framework of the company. You must get to know them, their aspirations, and who they are as a person. When I served as the vice president of US delivery operations I visited a business unit nearly every week. I started my day in the morning-loading operations where I would spend the first few hours speaking with employees and supervisors. My routine was to walk the lines with the managers of the operation in tow. I'd ask them to take me to their new employees and I'd interview those individuals. After giving the manager my cell phone, I'd ask them to record the session with video (after getting the employees' permission). The employees were often nervous. I would allay their fears and introduce myself to them. I let them know that the goal of the interview was for them to let me know how the job was going. I wanted to learn something about why they chose to work for UPS.

The interview questions were:

1. Tell me about yourself. What job did you have before UPS? (Employees typically gave me an overview of the job they had prior to UPS, if any.)

2. Why did you choose UPS? (These answers were generally due to the benefit package UPS offered or the hours of work selections being very compatible with their lifestyles. The long-term prospect for a career was also a common answer.)

3. Do you know the person holding my phone? (I would point toward the manager. This is when the education began for the managers. The employee would know their supervisor typically as they saw them daily. They almost never knew the supervisor's manager, the true person in charge.)

4. Who trained you? (They knew this about 50 percent of the time, as in many cases they had multiple trainers.)

5. How was the training? (The typical response to this question was "It was good." I would then say, "Can you show me what you've learned?")

The last thing I did was thank them for choosing UPS and introduce them to their manager. I then asked the manager and the employee to speak to each other for two to three minutes. I asked them to let each other know the names of their spouses and children, if any, and share what their favorite activities were when they had time off from work.

The intention of this exercise was to demonstrate to the managers and their team that knowing your people matters. Employees work for people, not companies. If you want employees to thrive, get to know them personally. The additional goal I had was for news to spread so that all operations would know I would do this exercise when visiting their operations across the US. The purpose of this was to intentionally get managers to engage and know their employees so that we would keep those we had hired.

To set an example I posted the videos weekly for the management team in the US to view.

This exercise inspired many of the managers to start their own interview and video-posting process. The point here is this: When you hire an employee, get to know the person. If you don't, your chances increase that they will fire you at some point.

EXERCISES

Build a template to interview your employees for ten minutes each. List these questions on it:

- How was your initial training?

- What would you improve?

- What are the five most-important things you want from the company?

- What are the five most-important things you want from me?

- What are some hobbies or activities you enjoy in your free time? (Reciprocate and share activities that you enjoy.)

CHAPTER TEN

DIRECTIONAL COMMUNICATION

I'VE FOUND THAT THE old saying, "It's not what you say, it's how you say it," is not completely accurate. Look no further than the world of social media and anger politics. A day doesn't go by in the headlines without some celebrity or politician trending on social media over a comment they have made. No matter how it was said, it was going to create issues for them. As a leader, what you say, how you say it, when you say it, and where you say it matters! In other words, it's not just the tone of the words you speak.

It all matters.

WORDS MATTER

Aaron Rodgers, the highly praised former quarterback

of the Green Bay Packers, learned this the hard way. During the pandemic, the NFL had to establish guidelines for the players based on their vaccination status. Players had to declare if they had been vaccinated or not. There were a number of players who chose not to be vaccinated and openly announced their position. Quarterbacks Kirk Cousins of the Minnesota Vikings and Carson Wentz of the Indianapolis Colts clearly told their teammates, the media, and their fans that they weren't going to get vaccinated. Their honesty on their decision had no impact for them on the field or with the media.

Aaron Rodgers, however, when asked at a press conference about whether he was vaccinated, said he had been "immunized." Eventually, people learned what he meant. Rodgers contracted the COVID virus. He had been using a home brew but had not been vaccinated. The criticism was swift from all angles. Ex-NFL players, the fans, and the media branded him a liar. Some of his sponsors such as State Farm Insurance, where he'd been a spokesman for years, dropped him. He lost credibility. He could have simply said, "I am choosing not to get vaccinated" as many had, and that would have been that.

DIRECTIONAL COMMUNICATION

He is one of the greatest quarterbacks to ever play the game, and so I am sure he would have kept the job. But he chose to wordplay, and accordingly, he lost something greater: people's respect.

The business world is not as forgiving as the sports world. If you say something that causes you to lose the respect of your boss, your peers, and, more importantly, your team, they won't support you, and it's possible you won't keep your job for very long. Again, it's not just the tone—words matter.

Your success as a leader will largely be driven by your communication skills. Surprisingly, many leaders ignore developing their verbal communication skills. Everyone—including leaders—needs a guide, a method, or an approach. I like to compare it to taking a road trip. Even with technology guiding your journey, you still need to use and recognize the signs you see along the road. Signs are meant to tell you how to proceed. There are street, exit, and traffic signs, along with street markers and lights, that guide your journey. If you were to ignore these signs, your chances of getting lost or having a crash would increase dramatically.

ADDRESSING NONVERBAL SIGNS OF DISAGREEMENT

Whether you are speaking to groups or an individual, there will be signs. You may see signs of acknowledgment and agreement, such as heads nodding affirmatively. The signs also could be eyes rolling, heads shaking in disagreement, or frowns. If you see negative signs and don't adjust the discussion, you could end up going in the wrong direction or crash. So you must adjust accordingly. Three steps needed to acknowledge these signs are:

1. Identify the individuals who disagree. Make a statement to the group, saying, "I can see that some of you have concerns." Acknowledging the signs is the most important step.

2. Let them know that you are willing to meet separately with those who want to express concerns.

3. Additionally, announce that once you have captured the concerns, you will inform the group of the concerns expressed and any adjustments as a result.

DIRECTIONAL COMMUNICATION

If individuals within the group become boisterous with their objections, calm them down. Keep control of the environment and state firmly that their concerns are important. You will ensure that they receive an ample opportunity to share them with you separately. What you cannot do as you maintain the respect of your team is to ignore negative signs.

We have a tradition each winter where my family and some of our extended family take a vacation to a ski resort. We always look forward to this trip; it's the one time during the year when we get to truly reconnect with one another.

One opportunity for this is when we ride the lifts together up the mountain slope. It takes ten minutes or so to ride the lift to the top, giving us a chance for conversation. On one occasion I was riding the lift with my sons, Pierce and Brayden. They began debating the impact and root causes of homelessness in Los Angeles. My older son, Pierce, at the time was twenty and was a member of a service group of all-male college students. They had recently completed a project where they were required to sleep outside on the streets without any funds to experience one night of homelessness. When Pierce spoke of that night, it was apparent the experience had been an emotionally moving one. In addition to sleeping on the streets, they spoke to people who were unhoused. That had given him a personal idea of the severity of their circumstances. In addition to that, Pierce also had a residency internship in Washington, DC, where he treated individuals who were homeless but were in the hospital. Therefore, his knowledge was attained through the close proximity he'd had with the homeless population.

I was sitting in between them getting the full impact of their argument, and I saw hazard signs flashing. Brayden's position on why people end up homeless conflicted with Pierce's position. Of course, my older son's recent experience provided him with more personal knowledge of the many dynamics surrounding the issue. Brayden had no proximity to the issue. He had not been homeless, nor had he been with homeless people. Neither son had any intention of modifying their position. At one point Pierce blurted out, "You're just stupid!" My younger son responded, "No, you're the one who's stupid!"

Neither son was paying any attention to the clear hazard signs: amplified voices and heads shaking in disagreement while the other was speaking. Each believed their view was the right view. This is common in discussions where two or more people are disagreeing and are passionate and unbending on their position.

At this point, I interjected and put up a stop sign by saying, "Time out guys!" They both grumbled, but the debate ceased after that. Pierce had crossed a line with his comment, and it resulted in a crash. **In debates, people generally don't see the line until they have crossed it.** Once that happens, productive discussion dies.

The views from the lift were breathtaking. So I said, "Hey guys, look at the view of the mountains to the left—isn't it awesome!" They both looked and commented that it was. Then I said, "And look to the right. The lake view is stunning!" They both agreed with that as well. I then said, "So here we are in the same place, and there are two views. You know it's possible to be in one place and have different views. Both can have merit, but you have to want to take the time to see and appreciate them both." I finished by saying, "There is more than one way to be right in most situations. There is rarely only one correct answer. The thing is that you won't see all those aspects if you are fixated on one view." They sat quietly and gave that some thought, and they didn't argue again—at least for the remainder of that trip!

When leading, you will be the conduit for communications from your company to your team. Everything your company wants your people to know will come to them through you, whether it's good news or bad news. This requires that you have the skills needed to bring about understanding and support for the message or direction. How you identify what style of communication a situation calls for is crucial.

There are one-on-one discussions, group discussions, daily messaging, discussions with employees about their performance, and conflict resolution situations. They all require a different set of skills. A key characteristic of the very best leaders I have known is their ability to use language masterfully. They know how to see the signs employees display moment by moment. They adjust to what they see and successfully guide the discussion. They know what to say, how to say it, and when to say it. It is obvious that they see conversation as a craft to be learned so it can be used as a tool. They particularly understand that they already know what their view is, yet they still want to listen closely to hear all of the other views.

I attended San Jose State and studied electrical engineering. During my freshman year I was recruited by IBM to be a lab intern. During the 1970s and '80s IBM was the leader in technology; companies such as Apple, Microsoft, and Google were not the giants they are today. This position required supporting engineers on the various projects at the time. This meant running tests and providing them with the resulting data. I was assigned to a group of thirteen engineers, and this is where I met Manfred Dreblow, an engineer from Russia. He had a deep Russian accent. He was reserved and kept to himself. This intimidated many of us interns. Manfred, who was in his fifties, was the most senior of the group. We often wondered why he was not the manager of the group as he was the most accomplished, having developed thirty-seven patents for IBM worth millions to the organization. He had a master's degree. Other engineers told us that Manfred had completed enough education to have three PhDs.

One day I arrived at work and walked by

Manfred's office. He beckoned me to come in and have a seat. I was surprised and quite frankly a bit nervous by the request, but of course I complied and sat down. He asked me what my goals were. What did I want to accomplish in life? My answers were typical for a nineteen-year-old engineering student: become an engineer and make a good living doing it.

"Smarts alone won't get that done. I would suggest you learn to communicate well," he advised.

He went on to say that in the world of engineering the smartest people almost never were the ones leading the group.

"There are a lot of smart people, but there are very few that are good at selling ideas and communicating them. Those that are, end up in the top leadership roles," he added.

Manfred used himself as an example. Even with all of his accomplishments at IBM, he felt he was never going to lead a group. He believed the language barrier and his deep Russian accent prevented him from leading. He had not invested in correcting his accent early enough in his career. He did not see the importance of being an excellent speaker early in his life, and he was urging me not to make that mistake.

DIRECTIONAL COMMUNICATION

I was not a poor speaker, but neither was I a polished communicator. There were, however, many brilliant engineers in the group, and I observed that the lead engineers all had effective communication skills. I had a science major and a science minor, and he suggested I might swap the latter for a communications minor. The next day I changed my minor to speech communications. It was one of the most important professional decisions I ever made.

It is one thing to have great ideas and thoughts, but getting others on board with them takes skill. This is where what you say, how you say it, and when you say it matters. Leaders must be strong communicators to be effective. I've met a slew of brilliant people with poor communication skills. They were poor at diction, selling ideas, and influencing people. They were great at developing a process or a technology solution, but it was obvious they didn't care about presenting it effectively.

To be great at anything requires first that you care enough to want to be great. Then you must actively invest in getting better at it. I consistently witnessed supervisors and managers who had invested very little in their personal communication skill development fail as leaders. It was also the one area that had the most impact on their results, good or bad. As a supervisor, you cannot overinvest time or energy in mastering this skill.

COMFORT MATTERS

When you are comfortable doing anything, it's because you're confident and so you do it better. I'd go a step further and add that being uncomfortable (lacking confidence) guarantees you won't do it well. Think about a pastime or a hobby, something you do a lot. Chances are you're probably pretty good at it because you feel comfortable doing it. As a leader there are two types of discussions you must be extremely comfortable (and not fear) doing in order to excel:

1. One-on-one discussions, which include areas such as training, discipline, and performance discussions
2. Public speaking

You should quickly identify whatever type of communication makes you uncomfortable. Once you know you are uncomfortable with it, you can work to become comfortable. I've always been struck by people who say they want to get better at communicating and then do nothing to hone their skills. Losing weight, eating better, saving money, whatever it is—to get better you first have to *want* to get better.

IDENTIFY WHAT'S HOLDING YOU BACK

One of my current mentees leads four employees in an accounting office. When we first met, as he was introducing himself, he was overusing what I call "fillers." His dialogue sounded something like this: "*Well*, Noel, *like* he *um like* wouldn't do what I was asking. *So* I *like...um* told him we *um* would need to speak. The employee then said he'd *um*, he would like some time, *um*, to think about it."

As I listened to him, I was more focused on his repeated use of *um* and *like* than on what he was saying. So I made our discussions going forward contingent on him eliminating two words from our future discussions: *um* and *like*. When you overuse sentence fillers, you appear unsure of what you are saying—because you are. This is one example of an area that was creating disruption in a person's communication. We all have *something* we can improve.

Manfred had a language barrier. That's just one communication barrier. I have witnessed other people who spoke much too fast, where others could not follow them, or they wouldn't let others get a word in edgewise. Then there are those who don't get to the point and take forever to tell you where they are going. When I encounter long-winded speakers, I use a metaphor, asking them, "Can you land the plane?" as a sign that I want them to finish. I smile and try to keep it humorous to avoid offending them.

PRACTICE, PRACTICE, AND THEN PRACTICE

Allen Iverson, the retired NBA player who was inducted into the Hall of Fame in 2016, was asked by a reporter after an intense game, "Allen, we've heard that you don't like practice. Can you speak to that?" Iverson responded with a line that is now infamous:

"Practice? *Practice?* You want to talk about *practice?* You don't want to talk about the game? You want to talk about practice!"

This line is frequently used by other athletes when the topic of practice comes up in any sport. Allen Iverson was a superstar, a once-in-a-generation talent, and he was dismissing the importance of practice. The media was not. All teams practice because practice leads to success. Iverson admitted later that he understood that practice matters. If you have played a sport or a musical instrument, you know the importance of practicing. Similarly, developing your ability to have one-on-one discussions with your employees requires practice.

You can't avoid practicing these skills and expect to be great at them. You will need to learn and master both quickly. Role-playing one-on-one situations and rehearsing is how you practice. There is a saying I mentioned earlier: "What you see, you remember. What you hear, you forget. What you do, you know." According to worklearning.com, we retain 20 percent of what we see, 30 percent of what we hear, and 90 percent of what we see, hear, and do. When we do something repeatedly, we retain it at a much higher rate.

EXERCISES

Now it's time to practice.

A. Ask a work peer, friend, or family member to assist you while you film yourself giving a small presentation. Pick a familiar topic to speak about, a hobby or something you enjoy. Identify what you would change in the way you present. Are you speaking clearly? Do you use too many fillers or take too long to get to your point? Is your pace appropriate? Can people follow along? Do you pause enough to let others comment? Answer these questions while you watch the recording.

B. Try filming and recording yourself in a conversation, using Teams, Google Meet, or Zoom. Are you missing nonverbal cues that someone is bored, having difficulty following, or is trying to speak but can't? What is your tone like? Is what you're saying accurate, truthful, and making a clear point?

CHAPTER ELEVEN

THE B.E.S.T. PRINCIPLE

When I was first promoted to a supervisor's position, I had a very binary approach when it came to employee performance. If the employee was doing the job, they could keep it; if they weren't, they should be let go. Of course, now I see that this approach was nonsensical at a minimum. Negative approaches to employees will and should be met with equally negative responses. When I was twenty, I had an employee whom I had been documenting regularly for underperforming. I was going to hold him accountable to the job while doing nothing to help him improve. The reviews of his work were never supportive or uplifting. After about two weeks of negative reviews, the employee spoke up.

"How I do in my job is a reflection of how you do in yours, right?" he asked.

"Yes," I replied.

"Well, why would I <bleeping> help you?" he asked.

What he said made perfect sense to me. I had done nothing to help him, so why would he help me? Today I look back at that moment and I see the face-palm emoji implying "Duh!" What was I thinking back then? The answer, of course, is that I *wasn't* thinking as a leader.

Fortunately, I had a manager, Glenn, who was excellent at communicating and training his people. When I reviewed the situation with him, he shook his head and asked me, "Why should he help you get better? You aren't helping him."

He then said, "Noel, your role is to make people better. Why else would we [UPS] need you? If everyone we hired was a star and did the job, we wouldn't need supervisors."

He went on to say, "Positive approaches create positive outcomes. Work with your people and develop them. That being said, go fix it."

That was my first lesson in realizing what my role was. Every supervisor will have a similar moment with an employee.

As a supervisor your role is to build up others, to develop them as employees and people. You can do one of two things as their leader: **You can encourage your people or discourage them—there is no third option**. Of course, you should never discourage them. I saw supervisors both new and experienced struggle with the fine line of accountability while maintaining positive employee relationships.

I was assigned to oversee a portion of the UPS internal Leadership Development School system in the mid-nineties. The curriculum was specifically designed for promoted managers and supervisors who had worked one to two years in their current role. This is where I was taught a concept known as the B.E.S.T. Principle. The B.E.S.T. Principle stands for **B**e clear, **E**xpect the best, **S**tick to the objective, and **T**est commitment. It was the first skill we required the attendees to learn. It is a discussion guidepost. The intention is to help the leader keep all discussions positive, focused, and developmental. Conversations with employees can often sway from the initial points. The B.E.S.T. Principle helps to "eliminate the sway." To do so, you need to:

BE CLEAR:
ALWAYS STATE THE EXACT GOAL AND PURPOSE FOR THE ENGAGEMENT WITH THE EMPLOYEE.

In a training scenario, what specific portion of the training will you be working on? What do you want the employee to get better at doing?

In a work discussion, why are you having the discussion? What are you specifically thanking or recognizing the employee for? If you are engaged in an improvement discussion, what specific area are you looking to help the employee improve (e.g., attendance, error rates)? You must *be clear* and leave no room for misunderstanding about the purpose of the discussion. This eliminates any assumptions being made. Maintain a positive atmosphere at all times.

The most critical step in "Be clear" is confirmation made by checking for common understanding. The employee must be able to state back to you the exact purpose for the engagement.

EXPECT THE BEST:
EXPRESS CONFIDENCE IN YOUR EMPLOYEES' ABILITY TO MEET THE GOAL.

The most important aspect of your relationship with your employees is that you show confidence in them and their abilities. If your comments are negative, or the way you treat them is degrading, employees will not get better! Nothing about directing negative comments toward the people you supervise makes sense. **If something doesn't make sense, then to the employee it is nonsense.** They will react negatively, which is appropriate. As their leader, what you say matters. When people feel valued, they feel motivated. Let them know you believe in them.

STICK TO THE OBJECTIVE:
DO NOT DEVIATE FROM THE
SPECIFIC REQUIREMENTS NEEDED.
KEEP THE FOCUS INTACT.

It was common for my two sons to point out each other's deficiencies. I would ask my older son, Pierce, to clean his room, and he would respond, "Brayden's room is dirty!" This is normal and expected behavior from those with whom you are looking for improvements. Employees can be experts in this approach. You cannot let the conversation deviate from the intended purpose. As they attempt to move you away from the topic, diplomatically and intentionally move them back to it. Remember: *Eliminate the sway.*

TEST COMMITMENT:
CHECK FOR UNDERSTANDING, FINALIZE, AND GET A VERBAL COMMITMENT.

Mutual understanding between you and your employees (or understanding the terms and conditions of the engagement) is essential. Why spend time in any discussion or activity if there is nothing to be committed to? Once you have completed the conversation or training, you must check for understanding by asking, "So what did we do or discuss today?" Then ask for a commitment from the employee to apply what was agreed on. This is the step most supervisors would shy away from. Practice this step until you are comfortable and master it.

Here is a simple example of the B.E.S.T. Principle in practice:

Be clear: "Good morning, Martin. Today we will work together to certify you on the proper methods needed to operate a forklift. There are sixteen specific steps required for you to complete the certification. So, Martin, can you tell me what we want to accomplish? Do you have any concerns?"

Expect the best: "I am confident that you have the ability needed to succeed in this training. I am here to support the effort I know you will put into this."

Stick to the objective: "Martin, as we go through each step, the ones you miss we will do until you are proficient. If you have any questions, ask. There are no bad questions. We will stay focused on the task until you are 100 percent certified."

Test commitment: "How does that sound, Martin? Can I have a commitment that you will apply yourself completely to becoming certified?"

The B.E.S.T. Principle is a frame with a blank canvas. You have to paint the picture, but it gives you, the supervisor, the ability to set a positive directional tone with your employees during all engagements. It gives you needed guardrails and keeps everyone on track during discussions. As you go through the other skills-training exercises in the book, the B.E.S.T. Principle should be incorporated into them.

EXERCISES

A. Teach someone—a friend, spouse, or partner—the B.E.S.T. Principle. Build a template with the four letters and their meanings.

B. Develop a few scenarios based on some common tasks around your home. Hold a discussion or training session with a friend, spouse, children, or partner using the B.E.S.T. Principle. Have your friend or family member critique your use of it.

CHAPTER TWELVE

THE 4X5 METHOD

For conflict resolution, the method I teach is known as the 3x5 method. I learned this method in the early phase of my career in a UPS leadership school where I was facilitator. Today there is no reference to the method that I can find. I have modified it to be the 4x5 method. This method is combined with the use of high-gain or open-ended questioning. It provides the supervisor with a map, a guide to help him or her adjust to the signs, positive or negative, and expressions of employees.

Your people see you loud and clear. Your *actions* regarding how others behave in your group sends a powerful message. There are *never* casual moments when leading a group. The axiom "Don't let your guard down" applies. If you let your guard down, you will get hit unexpectedly. The behaviors you allow ultimately become the terms and conditions within the group. As a leader you have to be prepared to expect the unexpected; the 4x5 method gives you the skills for exactly that. Situations come up, and when they do, they should always be handled in a professional, even tone. This structure helps you to accomplish that.

The 4x5 method is a situational approach to direct one-on-one conversations. There is particular emphasis on conflict resolution. In the story I referenced about my sons arguing on the ski lift, I wanted them to see that there is more than their own view. The number 4 referenced in the method represents the four types of viewpoints that can be taken in a work-related discussion. They are:

1. Your (the leader's) view
2. The customer's view
3. The company's view
4. The employee's view

The number 5 in the 4x5 method represents the five levels of intensity that can be used after identifying the specific issue. When having a discussion with an employee, it is the leader's task to consider which of the four viewpoints he will express and the correct point of view and level of intensity to use.

PICKING THE MOST EFFECTIVE POINT OF VIEW

The story about my two sons during our ski trip is an example of a discussion that had two viewpoints. Each of my sons had their own point of view (commonly referred to as a POV). As a leader you are not representing just your viewpoint; you also represent the company's and the customer's viewpoints. The front of the building I worked at never had a sign with my name on it. It wasn't called the Massie Company. I was leading on behalf of UPS to ensure that every customer got what they expected and what they paid for. When choosing a viewpoint in the 4x5 method, the perspective you choose is the one you believe will have the most *influence* on the employee's thinking and acceptance. So when choosing:

1. Your (the leader's) POV: You are saying "my personal perspective will have influence."

2. The customer's POV: You will help your employee

see the relevance of the customer's viewpoint, and that will have influence.

3. The company's POV: You will be using the company guidelines to influence the discussion.

4. The employee's POV: You will do your best to make the experience relevant to the employee in order to influence them.

WHEN TO USE VARIOUS VIEWPOINTS

Your viewpoint: Your viewpoint is the most preferable to launch a discussion when you are reinforcing your position on an issue, providing recognition, or reinforcing the terms and conditions you are upholding.

Customer's viewpoint: The customer's viewpoint is the most important of all viewpoints. Customers are the reason an employee has a job. Employees do inherently understand that, but still they often forget. When the customer's viewpoint is utilized, it reminds them who is paying for what they do.

Company's viewpoint: The company's viewpoint is the most favored in areas surrounding policies and procedures. These exist to protect the company and the employee, and they include areas such as safety protocols, workplace conduct, and policies designed to protect the company's brand and reputation.

Employee's viewpoint: The employee's viewpoint is the most effective of the four. It engages the employee in a discussion and in the solution. By engaging the employee in the solution, you have natural forces helping you because **people support what they help create.**

Ultimately, the viewpoint you use drives how you will start the discussion. You can and should use as many viewpoints in a discussion as possible. The employee's viewpoint when combined with the customer's viewpoint, for instance, has a powerful influence. How you start dictates the pathway you have decided to go down. Starting a discussion with any employee enhances that employee's self-esteem. **Regardless of the viewpoint you use, start the discussion by letting the employee know they are valued.**

Now that we have covered the four viewpoint choices in the method, let's look at the levels of intensity.

LEVELS OF INTENSITY/TONE

How you open a conversation—any conversation—dictates the success of that discussion. Even if you're doing something as simple as buying a donut in a donut shop, your level of intensity determines how the other person responds. For example, if you walk into a donut shop and there's a long line, and you yell at the counter employee, "I WANT A DONUT NOW!" you will probably be asked to leave the store. No donuts for you! In any discussion, tone and delivery of the message matter.

There are five levels of intensity that can be used during the course of any discussion. Level 1 is the lowest and level 5 is the highest.

These opening statements reflect the importance or tone with which you are approaching the issue. It allows you to size up the situation and predetermine or control your verbal response. Responding to an employee should always be professional and controlled, not emotional and unabated. I often witnessed supervisors using vocal amplification as their method of communicating intensity levels. Nothing could be more wrong. Words and vocal volume communicate tone.

DEFINITIONS OF EACH LEVEL

The opening statements that follow are meant to reflect the tone upon initial contact with the employee. This gives you a *feel* for how each level expresses itself to the employee.

Level 1: I *would like* to talk to you. This is a reserved level, nothing urgent here.

"Mike, when you get a moment, I *would like* to talk to you regarding some customer feedback."

Level 2: I *want* to talk to you. There's a bit more strength in that statement. You may want to understand or clear up an issue.

"Mike, I *want* to talk to you regarding some customer feedback." Using *want* indicates a stronger need to speak.

Level 3: I *need* to talk to you. This indicates that there is a clear need to talk; something important needs the employee's attention.

"Mike, I *need* to talk to you regarding the concerns from some of your customers." This lets Mike know that there is a problem that must be addressed.

Level 4: We *have* to talk. This level indicates there is a problem that must be corrected immediately.

"Mike, we *have* to talk today about some concerns from your customers." This level communicates that we have to repeat a discussion that we previously had.

Level 5: We *must* talk. This level is used when the problem is so severe that potential discipline may be forthcoming, or some issue is on the table that's nonnegotiable.

"Mike, we *must* talk today at 5:00 p.m. about some concerns from your customers." This statement or level is the highest and indicates the seriousness of the discussion.

In each case, the importance of the discussion was indicated by the opening statement, which telegraphs to the employee the tone of the issue, the urgency. Level 1 is indicating it's not an urgent matter. Level 5 indicates the matter is urgent and immediate attention is required. Mike's perception of urgency and importance, or the tone of the issue, comes from your approach or opening statement. *In no case should an amplification of your voice be the indicator.* Your statement itself should express the intensity level.

EXAMPLE OF A SUPERVISOR USING THE 4X5 METHOD

Paul was a supervisor who had twenty-five employees working for him and was about to address them prior to their heading to their assignments for the day. Just as Paul kicked off the meeting, one of his employees, Mark, noticed he was missing a day's pay when he looked at his paycheck. He began swearing, yelling, and having a full meltdown.

As Paul's manager at the time, I was standing some distance away observing the scene as it played out. Paul was a skilled supervisor and had excellent communication skills and techniques. He knew the 4x5 method and the nuances of it, and he was great at using it. He paused the meeting with the group and said, "Just a minute."

He walked over to Mark, making full eye contact.

"Mark, I *want* you to stop yelling and calm down. You are disrupting today's meeting with the group," Paul calmly said.

Mark continued with an amplified voice.

"You *need* to calm down. I will look into this for you immediately after I am done here. We are not going to solve this here and now; I understand you are upset and why. If you want to go sit in my office until I am done, then you may do that," Paul said, with more emphasis.

"If you stay here, you *must* not be disruptive," Paul then said firmly, without elevating his voice.

"OK," Mark solemnly replied.

The important aspect of this was that Paul handled a completely unexpected outburst from an employee in front of the team. He never lost control of the situation with his team or Mark. He controlled it completely and masterfully.

Once the group messaging ended, Paul took the employee to the office. He phoned the payroll department with the employee observing and the pay error was corrected. Once that was complete, Paul reviewed the behavior issue with Mark. He let him know that his behavior was inappropriate, and he was surprised by it. He had Mark commit to not repeating that behavior again.

Paul was good at handling these situations because he and his peers practiced the technique regularly. In baseball, as a batter hits a ball, you don't know where it's going. Practicing regularly teaches fielders how to judge quickly where it is going and field it. Paul moved quickly using the 4x5 method and fielded the issue. Let's unpack what Paul did.

1. Paul addressed the situation immediately to de-escalate it, pausing and moving the conversation away from the group. He walked over to the employee. He didn't speak from a distance and thereby made a more intimate connection.

2. He asked the employee to calm down using intensity level 2 by telling Mark that he *wanted* him to calm down. When that wasn't effective, he went to intensity level 3. He said, "I *need* you to calm down" while making eye contact with the employee. Finally, at intensity level 5, he told Mark that if he stayed there, he *must* not be disruptive.

3. He said, "I understand you are upset and why," thereby showing empathy to de-escalate the situation using the employee's point of view.

4. He made sure the employee knew what was not acceptable and stayed professional throughout the situation. He also got a commitment from the employee not to do it again.

Paul used the employee POV ("I will look into this for you") and intensity levels 2, 3, and 5. He was effective because he used a map (the 4x5 method), and as the signs on the road changed, he was able to navigate.

HIGH-GAIN OR OPENED-ENDED QUESTIONING

No one can be told to hold a view in which they do not believe. You can't just order your people to believe what you say and go with it. When you communicate to your team or an individual, they decide on their own if what you said makes sense. If it doesn't make sense, then to them it is *nonsense*! High-gain questions are intended to get the employee engaged in a discussion. They help you get the employee to speak, to contribute to seeing a certain perspective. Low-gain questions or set-up questions solicit answers such as yes or no. High-gain questions get the employee to think beyond their own perspective with the intent of influencing behavior.

Some high-gain questions include:

- Can you tell me what you like about flowers?

- Can you tell me what you think about the company's requirements for attendance?

- You just said John is your favorite customer. Can you tell me why?

High-gain questions are inserted in a discussion using set-up or low-gain questions. This drives the logic pathway. It moves the employee toward their own logical conclusion or solution. The key to an effective high-gain question is that it must lead the employee emotionally to see a different view and satisfy their "Why?" In other words, why should I change my view?

Simon Sinek, a notable motivational speaker, wrote the book *Start with Why*. It gives an excellent explanation on the premise and reasons for getting the employee's "why" satisfied. He argues, "Most organizations start with WHY, but only the great ones keep their Why satisfied year after year."[1] Sinek explains that we can't expect anyone to support an idea, a direction, or a conclusion before they understand the logic behind the requested change, or the *why*. His book explains that when you use high-gain questions, you must determine what why reasoning you will use.

Prior to asking a high-gain question, you need to set it up with a low-gain question opening. Using the preceding questions, we will set up opportunities to follow up with high-gain questions:

---

[1] Simon Sinek, *Start with Why: How Great Leaders Inspire Everyone to Take Action* (Penguin Books, 2011).

Low-gain question: What is your favorite flower?
Answer: Roses

It required a one-word response; therefore, it is low gain.

High-gain follow-up question: What do you like about roses? Or, why do you like roses? (There is usually a story from the employee attached to the question "why?")

Low-gain question: Do you like the company's policy on attendance?
Answer: No

High-gain follow-up question: Why don't you like the attendance policy?

Low-gain question: Who is your favorite customer?
Answer: Johns Supply Company

High-gain follow-up question: Why is Johns Supply your favorite customer?

The use of high- and low-gain questions, when combined with the viewpoint and intensity choices, help you build a map. You will use this map to get someone to go somewhere with you.

The actual discussion you'll have with an employee, whether preplanned or spontaneous, is what you'll need to *practice*. Over the years, I have used high-gain questions with the customer's and the employee's viewpoints the most frequently. Your intention in any discussion where there is a conflict or a problem to solve is not to have someone simply adopt your way of thinking. Your intention is to get employees to explore diverse ways of thinking and to develop or recognize a different view.

USE METAPHORS TO BRIDGE THE GAP

Metaphors are a powerful way to get employees to rethink an issue. It takes them outside of the current situation, depersonalizing and making it much easier for the employee to comprehend. Metaphors build bridges between your point of view and theirs. This is particularly effective when the chosen metaphor relates the situation to the person's own value system.

I use metaphors regularly. If there is an issue I want someone to see differently, my first thought is, *What metaphor can I use?* The very best metaphor I have found is when you can have someone use a personal experience that puts them in the other's shoes. In the earlier story with my sons on the ski lift, I used a metaphor. It defused the situation by asking them to consider the mountainside and lake—that everyone has a different "view." This depersonalized the situation and they were more willing to listen.

An individual's personal expectations are very consistent. When they buy something, they want what was paid for, reliability, and a fair exchange. This is a valuable tool when discussing uncomfortable issues with employees. Here are some examples of metaphors I have used with employees.

1. An employee is regularly absent or tardy.
A common metaphor I use for this issue is some kind of personal service that is universally used.

"Have you ever used Uber, Lyft, or ordered a taxi?" I ask.

Most employees say yes.

"Do you expect them to show up on time?" I ask.

"Yes, most of the time," is the most common

response. "I expect them around that time," a more forward-thinking employee might respond.

"So, then they get to show up whenever they want?" I ask.

"No" is the typical answer; however, employees recognizing where the discussion is going might not respond. This means the metaphor has succeeded early. "If they were always late or unpredictable, would you keep using them?"

"No."

I then turn the metaphor around on them. "What do we have to do to get you to be on time?"

This always ends with the employee saying, "I'll be on time."

If they continue to fail here, then who owns the outcome? The employee, of course. The key here is that the employee commits to improve something that makes sense to them.

2. An employee offers less-than-acceptable performance.

When work is shoddy, you find yourself informing the employee that their performance needs improvement and offer to assist them. They might get defensive or say they "don't care" about the company's work standards. They may even say the standards are arbitrary or impossible to meet. This is when a discussion in a private environment is more effective. Using intensity level 1 and employee point of view with a metaphor could sound like this: "Should any company have standards? If you take your car to be repaired, can they keep it for as long as they want? Or if your plumbing needs to be repaired, can they take as long as they want?" The employee never responds yes to these questions. These metaphors open the door for your discussion around standards.

3. An employee has an error rate of 5 percent; they are 95 percent effective. Your unit's goal is 99 percent.

You are working with the employee to improve to 99 percent, but they object. They believe 99 percent is unreasonable. You might say to the employee, "Have you ever had any work done, new roof, car repair, anything? If a roofer came and said, 'You know I'm a 95 percent roofer, so for every hundred shingles I lay, five will leak.' Would you hire them?" The employee always says no.

Another metaphor you might try in this situation involves a mechanic. "If you took your car for new tires and the mechanic said, 'Just want you to know we are 95 percent on tire installations. So, five out of every one hundred cars we put them on have a tire blow out while the car is being driven. However, we aren't responsible for any issues that arise because of it. Just want to know if you are good with that.' Would you buy from them?"

This disarms the employee and you can now focus on helping him or her to improve.

Disarming the employee by using a metaphor helps them see a different perspective. This makes your efforts toward improving their behavior or work more rational to the employee. They have to convince themselves on any issue that the behavior change being sought makes sense. The leader has to provide assistance getting them there.

In 2004 I received a call from a customer who was frantic about an item that had been lost. It was a custom-made German cuckoo clock. When she tracked the item, it indicated on the website that it had been delivered to her home. She said it had not and that she desperately needed it located. It seems that she had been saving it for thirty-five years and was planning to give it to her son.

She had purchased the clock right after she was married in Germany to commemorate the occasion. Her newly betrothed husband was in the US military and he was stationed in Germany. She became pregnant with their son shortly after they married. They were thrilled.

Unfortunately, the woman's husband was killed in Germany in an accident before their child was born. The cuckoo clock they purchased together took on an even greater meaning to her. So as you can understand, the item was irreplaceable. After hearing her story, I was committed to doing all I could to locate her item.

Jeff was the delivery driver who was shown as having delivered the item. He was an extremely diligent employee. I personally went to see Jeff and his manager to discuss the situation. I explained to them both what was at stake with the customer and the missing clock. Jeff felt terrible and said to me, "Noel, I am sure that if I had the clock, I delivered it to the correct address."

Here is how our conversation went step-by-step. I used intensity level 1 customer and employee viewpoint and low-gain questions, and a metaphor to create influence.

Step 1: Opening (Intensity Level 1)
Appreciation comment: "Jeff, I appreciate all that you do as an employee. I'd just like to ask you a few questions if you don't mind."

Step 2: Discussion (using low- and high-gain questions)
Low-gain questioning:
Me: You said you are 99 percent sure you took it to the right place?

Jeff: Yes.

Me: Alright, Jeff, I trust what you are saying.

Me: Jeff, she said she didn't get the clock. Do you have any reason to doubt her?

Jeff: No.

Jeff was visibly disturbed by the issue. He couldn't believe it was an issue on his side of things.

Jeff: Noel, I am pretty certain if the clock is lost that

I didn't have the clock—maybe the information is wrong.

Me: We have all been someone's customer, so let me ask you a question. You own a car. Have you had any work done on it?

He was surprised at my question, but he answered yes.

High-gain questioning:

Me: "When you bought the car, I'm sure having a warranty was an expectation. Can you tell me why?"

Jeff: "I would not have bought it otherwise. I wouldn't think it was reliable if they wouldn't give me a warranty."

Low-gain questioning:

Me: Jeff, what if the salesperson had told you, "You know, Jeff, we honor 95 percent of the warranties on our cars. So sometimes we sell a few that we won't honor the warranty on." Would you buy from them?

Jeff: No, I would not.

I did not have to continue. While I was speaking to Jeff, he was figuring out on his own where my questions were leading. He knew at this point that had we told the customer we could possibly lose the clock, she would not have relied on us. He had convinced *himself* that we needed to find that clock. He put himself in her shoes, which is the intent of using the employee and customer viewpoint when asking high-gain questions.

I asked Jeff if we could get his help locating the package. He replied, "I've got this. If I need help, I will let you know."

Jeff went back to the neighborhood after he was off work (which he was not required to do) and retraced his steps. He went door-to-door asking those on that street if they happened to have the clock, and finally, he found it! The address on the package said "Court," and he had delivered it to "Street" instead. Fortunately, the person who had the clock was honest and gave it back.

This was fifteen years ago. GPS technology has today eliminated this type of issue; it identifies for the driver exactly where they are. Jeff had no such support in 2004 and had delivered the package incorrectly. He took the package to the woman. She cried when he gave it to her. The following morning Jeff shared the experience with the peers in his group so they would not make a similar error. I thanked Jeff for his diligence in front of his peers. He felt good about correcting the error.

Low-gain questions are necessary; they steer the discussion. High-gain questions combined with metaphors are meant to influence the employee's thinking—to shift the employee's perspective so they see an issue or topic through their own eyes and the customer's. I've used these for most of my career because the process works the majority of the time. When an employee creates anything, they support it, particularly when they create an answer for themselves.

Can an employee always be swayed? No. There are some issues that an employee can feel so strongly about that their minds cannot be changed. During the pandemic that started in 2020, the Centers for Disease Control and Prevention (CDC) issued guidance on ways to protect yourself from being infected by COVID. There was no vaccine available during the first eight months. The recommendations were to wear a mask and socially distance at all times when around other people. Some people chose not to do this and could not be convinced otherwise.

Once a vaccine was developed, the recommendation was to get vaccinated and later to also get a booster shot. There were people who refused to do either. They had a set of beliefs they would not change. Many were prevented from entering establishments and flying on airplanes. Some even quit their jobs rather than comply. They could not be swayed to depart from their beliefs; it was a value for them.

In 1990 we at UPS were transitioning to a computerized device for deliveries. We were shedding the process of using a paper record with customers when they signed for a package. I witnessed, in one training session, two older drivers say they would *never* use a computer for their jobs. Both were above fifty-five years old at the time and both retired rather than use the device. We attempted to calm their fears. We demonstrated the device to them. We expressed how valued they were. It did not sway them. The point here is that the ability to influence someone's behavior through high- and low-gain question use has its limits. The one thing every individual can control every day is their own behavior and their beliefs.

EXERCISES

Consider these three hypothetical examples you might encounter as a supervisor.

1. One of your employees has developed an issue coming to work late in the last month. Previously they had a spotless record. They have been late to work five times in five weeks.

2. One of your employees has gone from doing his assignment at 100 percent daily down to 80 percent daily.

3. One of your employees was rude to a customer. You received a complaint.

Choose a viewpoint and a level of intensity for each, along with a metaphor. Choose someone to practice with on how you would open a discussion with an employee. Use low- and high-gain questions during the conversation. On a sheet of paper write out the intensity level choices and viewpoints. Give them to your practice partner. Refer to the sheet. State the view you will take and the intensity level you will use. Video record the session using a smartphone.

Now approach the occurrence of the employee being late a second, third, and up to sixth time. Debrief with your partner after each discussion. Did you sway them? Why or why not?

Create a series of situations that fit your workplace and practice them regularly with a partner.

CHAPTER THIRTEEN

DAILY MESSAGING WITH YOUR TEAM

I WAS ELECTED as chair of the board of the Los Angeles Chamber of Commerce in 2014. There is an annual dinner held to celebrate the chamber's accomplishments. That year there were approximately twelve hundred businesspeople in attendance. One of the many ceremonies during the banquet is the transfer of the gavel to the incoming chair from the outgoing one. The incoming chair is required to give a five-minute speech. The talk is an opportunity to thank the previous chair for his or her leadership and to present the new chair's areas of focus.

As the new chairman, I prepared to give my talk. As I looked out into the room, I saw people mingling and talking. The program had begun fifteen minutes prior to my taking the stage, and no one was paying attention. I went up to the microphone and announced to the room politely, "Can I have your attention please!" No one stopped what they were doing. I expected that. I then used an attention getter, announcing, "Servers, please serve no more alcohol for the next fifteen minutes." The servers stopped taking drinks to the tables. Everyone looked at the stage, surprised. However, they were now focused squarely on me. I had definitely captured their attention!

My next comment was to ask for applause for our prior chair for his accomplishments. After the applause, I thanked all of them for their continued support for the Los Angeles Chamber of Commerce. I then told them that over the next five minutes, I would cover what was accomplished last year and what would be our priorities for the coming year. I reviewed both topics and summarized by saying, "I have reviewed last year's accomplishments and went through each again." And then I reviewed the year's goals once more point by point. I thanked them again for their future support. The talk lasted just under five minutes. I closed by delivering the happy news that the servers could now begin serving drinks.

Everyone clapped at that announcement, of course!

In an average year as a business unit president, I visited one hundred and fifty to two hundred businesses. These included a variety of companies, from giants such as Costco, McKesson Corporation, and CVS down to small companies with two hundred or fewer employees. I met with their leaders to check on how we (UPS) were doing for them.

During my visit I observed their operations. It was rare not to see three- to five-minute team-based daily talks being given at the start of the workday. Also, senior management and small business owners had one consistent expectation: that all strategy objectives, all regulatory compliance requirements, and *all* communication to employees were done by their immediate managers or supervisors.

I had the same expectation as a president of my frontline teams. UPS knew that daily communication talks were important and invested in the expense, as did Walmart, Home Depot, and any large organization. For UPS, the cost of giving such three-minute talks is about half a million dollars *per day*. That's approximately 280,000 hourly paid employees at thirty dollars an hour, which equated to 14,000 hours a day of payroll allocated for daily communications.

Additionally, many companies invest in communications leadership to craft the daily messages that need to be delivered to employees. UPS had a president in charge of an entire organizational structure dedicated to the morning communication messages. More than one hundred trained and specialized individuals craft these messages based on what is important and timely.

Why was this investment made? There are many reasons, one being to eliminate the risk that arises when you have no or poor daily communication. Employees need to know what the company's priorities are, every single day. Also, you never know who is going to show up at your front door. It was common for inspectors from the Occupational Safety and Health Administration (OSHA), the Department of Transportation (DOT), the Federal Aviation Administration (FAA), and state regulators to come and quiz employees on anything and everything. These three- to five-minute team-based daily talks are used to provide important information, recognition, education, and training.

Ultimately, this kind of instructional communication protects frontline employees and the company. Amazon and Walmart, two companies with over a million employees, are paying upward of two million dollars a day for similar meetings. CEOs and all presidents at UPS call this the most important three minutes of the day.

As a leader, you will be the conduit that provides this daily messaging to your team. Typically, you will give these three- to five-minute talks daily on topics such as changes in policy, work rules, emergency plan instructions, safety tips, and daily work assignments. You also will be expected to provide this communication in an effective manner. Anytime you communicate with your team, you want to ensure they understand you and can be observed responding to what you are telling them during the meetings and throughout the workday.

Not all talks are equal. Some messages may require basic information to be relayed. Other messages you deliver may be more detailed and will require more gravitas and diligence. For example, a boss may spend the first minute speaking about where the weekend company picnic will be held, a message that does not require a strong, precise delivery. This individual may then be tasked with explaining an intricate new mechanical procedure or update on company policy. These explanations require clear and articulate communication. When you have an important message to deliver, you can't deliver it casually.

Every time you are delivering a message to a team, you're either informing, educating, or training. Scientist Siegfried Engelmann, director of the National Institute for Direct Instruction, said, "If the student hasn't learned, the teacher hasn't taught—that's not a slogan, it's an operating principle."[1] This applies to leaders' timed teaching moments as well.

Your team *will* make assessments of you based on their observation of your abilities. Being professional when addressing them, being prepared, and having a smooth delivery takes practice. You may be casual in dress and demeanor and at times be humorous with your team. Just remember there is no moment so casual that you are not being evaluated.

I often watched supervisors address their teams

---

[1] S. Barbash, "Science in the Service of Humanity: The Astonishing Contributions of Siegfried Engelmann," *Perspectives on Behavior Science* 44 (2021), https://doi.org/10.1007/s40614-021-00293-z.

at meetings prior to the beginning of employee assignments. I could tell what level of respect the group had for that leader by observing if employees were paying attention or not. When the leader was respected, employees looked directly at him or her. When the supervisor was structured and professional, the employees retained the message.

When the supervisor was casual and undisciplined, it was obvious the team was distracted and didn't respect them. Employees at those meetings often looked at their phones, engaged in small talk, or had quizzical looks in their eyes. The message was lost.

Frequently after observing a meeting, I would approach the employees and ask, "What did you think about what your supervisor just covered?" Employees with disciplined leaders could repeat what they heard. Those with unstructured leaders could not repeat the message.

Those who were most successful at delivering these talks followed a specific and easy-to-replicate structure that I've worked with in several roles. One of the most proven methods in helping knowledge retention is to repeat the key learning point at the beginning, middle, and end of a talk. This technique helps the employee remember the information.

But there is more to the structure than that. Remember the earlier quote supported by worklearning.com? What you see, you remember. What you hear, you forget. What you do, you know.

I was assigned to help develop the curriculum for UPS Leadership Schools with the Forum Corporation headquartered in Boston. They constantly reinforced the concept that people retain approximately 20 percent of what they hear, 30 percent of what they see, and well above 90 percent of what they do. This is based on the Cone of Experience created by Professor Edgar Dale, an influential American educator. While this can vary by individual, the key point is that the retention rate of information will be influenced by the presentation choice. When giving a three- to five-minute instructional talk, simply speaking to employees will capture the low end of the retention rate. You can't just read the memo. As a leader, seeing your role solely as informing or directing minimizes your importance. Strong leaders are strong educators and trainers, and they are development oriented. When you make a presentation to your team, these are some keys to success:

A. **Be clear.** Speak clearly and enunciate properly. Focus on your diction. Don't use word fillers such as *um*, *ah*, *like*, and *you know*. These are distracting. People will focus more on the fillers than the message.

B. **Be concise.** Don't ramble. Only include information specific to the topic you are covering.

C. **Be specific.** Cover each point of importance in succession: A, B, C, and so forth. Use visual aids to support the message, where the opportunity exists. What people see, they remember.

D. **Check for understanding.** Look for signs of confusion or distraction, including frowns or quizzical expressions. If you notice these, ask, "Would anyone like a key point covered again?"

DAILY MEETING SCRIPT TEMPLATE

Here are the five key parts of an effective daily message, listed in order as steps:

STEP 1: THE ATTENTION-GETTER

This should take no longer than thirty seconds. It could be a short story that relates to your topic. It could be employee recognition, which is always a wonderful place to start. This may include acknowledgment of somebody doing a good job, having a birthday or an anniversary, or the birth of a son or daughter. The options are endless. Once you have their attention, you can proceed to step 2.

STEP 2: TELL THEM WHAT YOU'RE GOING TO TELL THEM

In this step, you preview the topic you will discuss. Be specific and clear. You are covering the "why" with the group and explaining your *purpose* for reviewing the topic. For example, you might say, "Today I am going to cover emergency procedures. During an emergency, it is important that you understand for your safety what the requirements are and where to go immediately." Then integrate bullet points—that is, what you will cover:

- What to do in the event you hear a siren.

- Where you should assemble during a building evacuation.

- How to know when an all clear has been given.

This, of course, would be customized to the message you'll be delivering that day.

STEP 3: TELL THEM

This is the body of your talk. Again, *be specific, be clear, be concise.* In this portion of your talk develop the key points that were previously covered. **The use of visual aids gives you a significant retention advantage. (Remember: What people see, they remember.)** This is where you will elaborate on your content. For example:

- **What to do in the event you hear a siren.**

The facility is equipped with sirens. When you hear these sirens, you are to evacuate the facility immediately. No matter what you are doing, you are to exit. Asking questions such as "What's happening?" or looking for information delays your exit and is unsafe.

- **Where you should assemble during a building evacuation.**

Each workgroup is assigned a specific location for assembly. Our workgroup's location is indicated on the diagram I am handing out to you. As you can see, you are to assemble outside in the far north corner of the parking lot. I will be going there as well, so you can expect to see me in that area.

- **How to know when an all clear has been given.**

Once we are in the emergency assembly area, I will update you on all known details. You are to remain in the area until I have been given the all clear. Only then may I release you. This is for your safety. For example, if a toxic chemical has been released, you are to remain here until we know what it is.

STEP 4: TELL THEM WHAT YOU TOLD THEM

You will summarize what you have covered in the order in which you reviewed it. This is where message retention is reinforced:

- What to do in the event that you hear a siren.

You are to evacuate immediately and not ask for information about what is going on.

- You are to assemble in the far north corner of the parking lot. I will meet you there.

- The all clear will be given to me when it is safe to release you. Remain in the area until then. This is for your safety.

STEP 5: CHECK FOR UNDERSTANDING

Ask someone in the group, "What did we cover today?" Let them state what they learned. This is a good litmus test for you. It lets you know how effective you have been. It is better to know earlier before confusion really sets in and you recognize employees didn't learn.

When I observed meetings, when an employee missed something, I would often hear supervisors say, "Well, I covered that topic with everyone." I never allowed a supervisor to assign blame to the employees for not knowing. I am sure your company won't either.

Once you have wrapped up the meeting, let employees know that if they need further clarification, you can review it again one-on-one. There is always someone with a question. This will ensure they are comfortable afterward asking it.

The key to setting solid terms and conditions among your team is to always be a professional example. Delivering effective daily talks helps you do that. This is not to say you need to be robotic—quite the opposite. By using your attention getter and starting the day on a positive note, you are setting a human tone.

Conversely, when you fail to deliver messages professionally, you are also setting a tone. I used a building evacuation for my example—which could become a life-or-death situation in a real emergency if an evacuation occurred and an employee hadn't retained the information; the leader may be held responsible. They are your team. Who should own how much they know?

EXERCISES

Develop an emergency plan for your family, roommates, and so forth. Use your most common potential natural disaster: a hurricane, tornado, earthquake, severe weather. Build a three- to five-minute talk to deliver about steps to take if one of these events takes place. Be sure a colleague, family member, or friend times you. When you're finished, get their feedback on your talk. Practice until your talk is under five minutes and your audience reacts positively.

CONCLUSION

There was a position open to be a leader, and you held your hand up and said, "Pick me! Pick me!" Well, you were picked. Now the real work starts. Leading effectively day-to-day takes thought and preparedness. When I was promoted to my first true leadership position, I had no idea what the position would look like or what would be expected of me. Most new leaders don't. I've had hundreds of conversations throughout my career with leaders who wondered within a year of being promoted if they had made the right decision. I always encouraged them and let them know that if they did not possess the talent, they would not have been chosen. You were chosen. You obviously have the talent.

The rigors that come with a leadership position aren't always obvious from observing other leaders. As the manager for US operations at UPS, one of my most-significant challenges was keeping pace with frontline leadership training demands. I wrote this book to provide those fairly new to leadership with a starting point. It is not intended as the be-all and end-all—there is no such thing when it comes to leadership development. That is true in any profession, and leadership is a profession. To be great you must commit to learning and growing constantly.

"Things are different today" is a common statement you'll read in journals, books, and articles on leadership. I heard it often from supervisors when I participated in roundtable discussions with them throughout the US. Sure, things are different today, and they will be different tomorrow, and the day after that as well. That's as obvious a statement as saying water is wet.

When I was promoted in 1980 things were different than in the generations that had passed—and thank goodness for that! What my generation wanted was different from the generation before us. Each generation always improves on the last. Leaders who use approaches and techniques that fail to keep up with generational change eventually fail. They fail to adapt, they fail to grow, and ultimately this turns into a lack of success with their teams.

CONCLUSION

The changes I witnessed over my six-decade career could fill a book all by themselves. The most obvious change I've recognized is that tolerance levels for accepting poor treatment from leaders has consistently gone down. If today's employees' terms and conditions are not met, they will quit on the leader.

Elon Musk, who some say has achieved legendary status as a leader, has proven this case at X (formerly Twitter), which he purchased in 2022. He announced to the employees within days of buying the company that he would be making numerous changes within the organization. Many of the employees objected to what they were hearing, so scores of highly talented professionals just walked out…on Elon Musk! The obvious reason they walked was that their terms and conditions to stay had not been met.

The influence of social media presents the greatest change and challenge that any organization has ever witnessed. It brings with it a transparency to all things that happen in society and in the workplace. Transparency is now expected, and if it is not provided by the leaders, an employee will ensure that it is on social media. What might have seemed a small thing can become a massive thing—quickly. Lives can change instantly as a result. These changes require adaptation. They also require awareness and an approach that keeps all of the lines straight between the employee and the leaders. By adhering to the terms and conditions of leadership, you can navigate these changes.

Yes, generational values and norms do change; however, some principles do not change. In leadership there are certain principles that cut across generations and always apply. For employees to provide discretionary effort in their work to help the organization succeed, they must feel valued. When they do not, the company does not get better, nor does your team.

Leadership is a professional discipline—as with any discipline it has to be learned. It is not a simple science. It is important to understand early in your career that there are some techniques that you can use to set a values-based tone with your team. Employees from diverse backgrounds with different belief systems will enter into conflicts with one another on the job. There will be dissatisfaction with company policy and changes. How you approach these issues

CONCLUSION

and lead through them requires practice.

The number one reason I saw failure in leadership were individuals not respecting what it takes to excel. Accepting the position and then believing you're smart enough, that you work hard enough, or that you are educated enough is a good start; but those things alone are not enough. **You are always being evaluated—always.** Your opinion of your work matters, but it is the *least* important opinion. Your people's opinion of your leadership is the most important thing, as their opinion is the most accurate.

The terms and conditions of leadership are the ways in which you set the tone with your team that you are there for one reason: to support *their* success. You can't do that if you are self-centered or if your ego or pride gets in your way, so don't let them.

Developing the skills discussed in this book will help guide you on your journey. The value equations—integrity, ethics, fairness, and listening to others—are key ingredients to building trust. Without them you cannot build trust. It's that simple. The skills needed in part two have to be practiced and rehearsed repeatedly for as long as you are a leader. Whether you are a supervisor or a CEO, skill development never ends until you stop getting on the field daily.

In Stephen Covey's book, the second habit of highly effective people is "begin with the end in mind." Successful leaders know what they want the end view to look like. As you begin your career, how do you want to be viewed? What do you want those you have led to think of you? How do you want your peers to view you? What do you want your legacy as a leader to be?

When I was a manager there was a significant dispute between the union business agent and the company. He filed a formal grievance. He later wrote a letter to withdraw the grievance. It was addressed to the head of labor relations and the president of the area at the time. He stated he would withdraw the grievance only if I would be left in place as the leader of the unit I was assigned to. In the letter he wrote, "Noel Massie as a manager is fair to all employees and union personnel. Even when it did not benefit the union or employee, which has earned him the respect of all who he has come into contact with." The president of the district called me and thanked me. It is a phone call I will never forget. I still have a copy of that letter. When I began, I wanted to be known as a fair leader. I wanted my legacy to be defined by my fairness and treatment of all workers, regardless of their station, rank, gender, race, or age. Despite the fact that I made a few mistakes, I believe I accomplished this goal.

My point in sharing this is not to toot my own horn; rather, it's to convey that you really do get to control your personal values, attitude, and actions. These become your legacy.

The manner in which employees provide service to the customers who choose to buy from a company is an extension of how these employees are treated by their leaders. Employees who provide excellent service to their customers do so as a result of having a leader who serves them. The number one question I would ask employees, individually or in a group, was, "How often should you do the right thing?" The answer I would get was, "All the time." It was impactful and it held us all accountable, particularly me. I had to serve them in order for them to serve the organization—that just made sense. The plaque shown here was bestowed on me by the group of employees in the photograph. It remains one of the greatest honors I have been given.

CONCLUSION

Remember, there are always terms and conditions in leadership and life. Leaving a legacy you can be proud of starts with these.

So, what do you want your legacy to be? What are the terms and conditions that will define your leadership legacy? Your life? You, and only you, get to decide those, so make sure you review and write your own fine print!

ACKNOWLEDGMENTS

THE DECISION to write this book for newly promoted leaders came to me over ten years ago. This was primarily due to the promotion of so many new leaders in our company as baby boomers were retiring. It was also due to the economic conditions of that time as many companies looking to cut costs were reducing their training budgets. Unfortunately, those budgets are always the first to go. When speaking to my peers across other Fortune 500 companies, they reinforced that this is the trend in their companies as well.

Considering something and doing it are two completely different activities. I would not have gone forward to write this book without the encouragement I received from many. Matt Toledo, previously the president of the *Los Angeles Business Journal* and Renee Fraser, PHD and CEO of Fraser Communications, are just two who influenced the writing of this book. Additional motivation came from some UPS leaders

ACKNOWLEDGMENTS

who were members of my senior staff, including Kellie Aamodt, Derrick Waters, Nick Kocheck, Lou Riveccio, Stan Deans, John Greaves, and Joe Boyle. All are strong UPS leaders who, once I mentioned my intentions, encouraged me to complete this effort. They joined my commitment to developing young leaders, and I want to thank all of them for their input.

My professional career taught me that working with experts in any field is the best path to learning what you don't know. In this regard I was fortunate to meet Blake Pinto, a consummate professional. Along with developing my website and media, he provided me with the knowledge I needed to network to the right people. It was through him that I met the most important person in this journey—my book coach, Mary Curren Hackett. She has been a teacher, friend, and mentor. I was incredibly fortunate to meet Mary. It was inspiring to have the opportunity to learn how to put thoughts on a page and be an author from her.

Finally, I want to acknowledge the Brand Builders Group. It has been insightful and rewarding to work with their team of professionals. Rory and AJ Vaden have created a platform to help novice authors

ACKNOWLEDGMENTS

navigate the world of publishing, which can be confusing and complex. Their contribution is what took this book over the finish line.